MW01231525

KINGDOM AUTHORITY

EXERCISING GOD'S RULE IN YOUR LIFE

DR. TONY EVANS

B&H
PUBLISHING
BRENTWOOD, TENNESSEE

Published by B&H Publishing Group
Brentwood, Tennessee

Dewey Decimal Classification: 231.72
Subject Heading: GOD / SPIRITUAL LIFE /
KINGDOM OF GOD

Unless otherwise noted, all Scripture quotations
are taken from the New American Standard Bible (NASB),
copyright © 1960, 1962, 1963, 1968, 1971, 1972, 1973,
1975, 1977, 1995 by The Lockman Foundation.

Cover design by Edward Patton.
Crown art by pingebat/shutterstock.
Author photo by Pharris Photos and Philms.

1 2 3 4 5 6 • 27 26 25 24 23

Acknowledgments

I would like to thank Lifeway Christian Resources and B&H Publishing for their long-standing relationship in publishing, events, and film. It is always a joy to get to work on a project with such Spirit-led servants of the King. I especially want to thank Bill Craig for shepherding this relationship over the years. I also want to thank Mary Wiley and Kim Stanford for their work in reviewing and laying out this manuscript. Lastly, I want to thank Heather Hair for her continued dedication to my written library through her collaboration on this manuscript.

Contents

Bringing Heaven to Earth

 If you have satellite TV, then you receive programming from space onto your TV screen through your receiver. Without a receiver, the programming that is available to you cannot be accessed. If you have a receiver but it is turned off, then you still cannot experience the available programming.

Non-Christians do not possess the Spirit of God, so they have no receiver to access spiritual realities for their lives (1 Cor. 2:14). Believers, on the other hand, possess a receiver (1 Cor. 2:15–16) but may not have it on so that they can access heaven's authority for use in the divine programming for their daily lives. They have the Spirit, but are not attuned to Him but to the flesh instead, resulting in powerlessness and defeat when it comes to exercising kingdom authority on earth (1 Cor. 3:1–3).

Even if the receiver is working, it is Satan's goal to create static and spiritual disruption so that the signal is blocked, keeping us from clearly receiving heaven's answers to earth's realities and fulfilling our destiny. Like a storm that disrupts TV programming causing the screen to go blank and advertise "searching for signal," our archenemy is forever seeking to keep us from understanding and experiencing all the rights and privileges that are ours as sons and daughters of the Most High God. The result is that believers are left discouraged, defeated, hopeless, powerless, and purposeless.

When God created mankind, it was His intended purpose to partner with the human race to bring His will from the spiritual realm into the physical realm. So, He turned the managerial operation of earth over to mankind when He said "Let them rule" (Gen. 1:26). The stewardship of the planet then would be in the hands of humanity (Ps. 115:16).

God simultaneously gave men the responsibility to choose whether or not they would rule under His authority. Their obedience, faith, and submission to His Word would empower them to successfully exercise dominion in and over His creation. This authority was immediately implemented when Adam was given the right to name all the animals. God brought them but Adam named them. Thus, the scope of man's kingdom authority would be determined by his cooperating with what God wanted done, not simply by what he wanted to do.

Therefore, kingdom authority is to be directly tied to accomplishing the will of God as human kind lives by divine revelation, not human reason (symbolized by the prohibition against eating from the google tree of the knowledge of good and evil). However, man's disobedience led to the transfer of his God given authority over to Satan (Gen. 3:1–24; 1 John 5).

However, when Jesus arose from the dead He reclaimed mankind's God given right to rule (Heb. 2:14; Eph. 1:1, 18–19) and proclaimed kingdom authority in both heaven and earth (Matt. 28:19–20). He would personally serve as the link between eternity and time and between the spiritual and the physical (Matt. 28:18; Eph. 1:10; Phil. 2:10). It is God's goal to transfer authority from heaven into history through His kingdom disciples who consistently live all of life under Jesus's lordship (Rom. 14:8–9; Matt. 28:19–20). He occupies the executive seat of authority in heaven (Eph. 1:20) and gives us the privilege to sit beside Him (Eph. 2:6) so we can share in His position of authority. This authority is realized and activated as Jesus equips His followers to rule on His behalf as we overcome this world's attempt to defeat us.

However, while kingdom authority is provided to all believers, it is not a guaranteed experience. The desire of this work is to inspire and equip believers to embrace the right to rule God offers to His people so we live out our divinely designed purpose and kingdom calling.

Kingdom authority gives believers, both individually and collectively as the church, the authorized right to exercise kingdom authority in order to bind and loose (i.e., forbid or permit—Matt. 16:18–20; Luke 9:1–2) when we are in spiritual agreement with

God. The goal of kingdom authority is to obtain divine resources and support from the invisible realm into the visible realm. It is time for believers to exercise our kingdom constitutional right to act as heaven's representatives on earth since it is the Father's good pleasure to give us the kingdom (Luke 12:32).

CHAPTER ONE

The Key

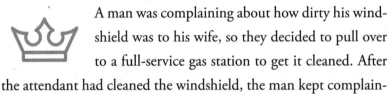 A man was complaining about how dirty his windshield was to his wife, so they decided to pull over to a full-service gas station to get it cleaned. After the attendant had cleaned the windshield, the man kept complaining. "It's still dirty," he said. "Have him clean it again."

The man's wife rolled down her window to call the attendant back over to clean the windshield again. The attendant shrugged his shoulders, mumbled something under his breath, and then went about cleaning the already clean windshield. This time when he had finished, the man sighed deeply. "It's still dirty," he said. "Maybe I should get out and clean it myself!"

As he put his hand on the door handle to get out of the car, his wife leaned over to touch his arm. "Just a second," she said. "Hand me your glasses."

The man decided to listen to his wife and hand her his glasses. That's when she wiped his glass lenses clean and then handed them back to him. When he put his glasses back on, he could see that the windshield of his car was spotless. The problem had been his glasses all along. He had thought the problem was something else when really, *he* was the problem. He could not see clearly through the mess on his own glasses. And because he wasn't seeing clearly, his perspective had become jaded, and his attitude had become frustrated with everyone else around him.

Paul addressed our spiritual perspective and how it relates to our kingdom authority when he wrote to the Christians at Ephesus. He told them, in a manner of speaking, that they need to start putting on some new glasses. Far too many of us are like the believers at Ephesus and could use a new pair of glasses ourselves. We miss out on accessing what God has for us because we fail to tie our shaded and messed-up view with that which blocks us from experiencing all God has to offer.

God desires for each of us to live with kingdom authority. For starters, the kingdom agenda is *the visible manifestation of the comprehensive rule of God over every area of life.* Thus, kingdom authority can be defined as *the divinely authorized right and responsibility delegated to believers to act on God's behalf in spiritually ruling over His creation under the lordship of Jesus Christ.* In short, it's yours and my legitimate right to rule underneath Jesus's rule.

Yet so many individuals miss out on fully exercising this right to rule simply because they do not know or are not utilizing the key to unlocking it. They do not know the key because they cannot see the key. And they cannot see the key because they are not seeing things spiritually. Christians who are living in defeat are doing so because they are not seeing things clearly. In fact, all of us—to varying degrees—have worn jaded-colored glasses at some time or another. That's why we need to pay attention to Paul and what he has to say to the church at Ephesus. We need to learn from what he had to say to these believers because part of participating in God's rule on earth comes through learning how to see things spiritually.

Paul wrote this passage to clarify the believers' sight lines. He wanted to clean the glasses they were wearing, and ultimately the glasses we are wearing as believers as well—or, if necessary, help us to get to new ones. For kingdom followers to unlock their kingdom authority, it is imperative that we first see things clearly. When we discover how to see things clearly from a spiritual framework, we will grab hold of the key to the authority we so desperately need. Paul seeks to enlighten us when he introduces this subject in Ephesians 1:15–19 by saying,

> For this reason I too, having heard of the faith in the Lord Jesus which exists among you and your love for all the saints, do not cease giving thanks for you, while making mention of you in my prayers; that the God of our Lord Jesus Christ, the Father of glory, may give to you a spirit of wisdom and of revelation in the knowledge of Him. I pray that the eyes of your heart may be enlightened, so that you will know what is the hope of His calling, what

are the riches of the glory of His inheritance in the saints, and what is the surpassing greatness of His power toward us who believe.

Paul's desire for the believers in Ephesus was that they would start seeing things as they really are, and not as they think they are. He wanted God to clarify things for them. In today's culture, you might hear people refer to this as "waking up." When someone tells you to "wake up," they are stating they want you to see things clearly and not be duped by the deception all around us.

Paul wanted the believers to "wake up" and see through spiritual eyes. He wanted this so much that he prayed for this to happen. He knew they could not wake up on their own. He knew they could not strip the scales of Satan's deceit with their own hands. Paul prayed that the eyes of their hearts would be illuminated because something that deep would need to happen supernaturally. They needed their eyes opened to gain insight into both the position and authority they already possessed. If they didn't, they would certainly cave to the culture around them.

That's why Paul's prayer ought to be each of our prayers as well. Our culture, and those who nuance it, are hell-bent on creating confusion in the lives of believers—or in the lives of anyone, for that matter. So much deception swirls around us that it is difficult to tell up from down or left from right on most days. The first step to unlocking and unleashing God's kingdom authority in our lives is through praying regularly to God, asking Him to help us see and interpret things spiritually. We need His perspective and wisdom so we can recognize the truth from a lie.

In fact, Paul used an interesting word at the end of verse 18 when he spoke about what the believers needed their eyes opened to see. He had prayed that their eyes would be opened so they could see "what are the riches of the glory of His inheritance in the saints." In a time when the believers at Ephesus no doubt struggled with lack, opposition, and loss, Paul had the courage to call them "rich." This is because, from a heavenly perspective, they were. What's more, so are we. So are you.

It's true. You and I are rich in the spiritual realm because of what we have inherited by virtue of our faith in Jesus Christ. No matter how you may feel or how desperate things may seem, there exists no poor person spiritually as far as our inheritance is concerned. You and I have access to all we need in the spiritual realm. What understanding and unlocking kingdom authority does is helps enable us to draw that down into the physical realm in which we live right here and now. Thus, if you are spiritually poor—or even circumstantially, relationally, or emotionally poor—it is not because of a lack of provision by God. He has made every good and perfect gift available to us as His followers (James 1:17). Rather, if you are not living out the fullness of these gifts, it is because of your inability to tap into the spiritual inheritance He has for you. It's due to your lack of accessing His kingdom authority—something I'm hoping you will learn how to do more completely as we go through this book together. But, for starters, I want you to know I

understand it's hard to access something you don't even know you
have. That's why our eyes need to be opened.

Like many of you, I fly American Airlines. I speak frequently,
pretty much weekly, at other locations, or I will often travel to film
a Bible study or something for our ministry, so I have accumulated
a lot of miles over fifty years. As a result, I'm now an executive
Platinum flyer. As an executive Platinum flyer, I get a book in the
mail every year that gives me details on all of the rights and privileges I get to access because of my relationship with the airline.

But, to be honest, I really haven't paid much attention to that
book over the years. Every time I would get it, I would usually
thumb through it and then toss it in the recycling bin. I didn't pay
much attention to it because I was only concerned with one thing
when it came to American Airlines: I wanted them to get me from
Point A to Point B and upgrade me if possible. That's pretty much
all I cared about. Just safely fly me from here to there and I'm a
happy camper.

But recently I decided to thumb through my book of rewards
more closely. That's when I discovered there were quite a few rights
and privileges I had accrued that I had failed to take full advantage
of. In fact, I discovered I had a number of completely free flights I
could take! All I had to do was ask for them. This made me pause
because I had often taken a flight to see family members or friends
on special occasions and had paid for it myself. But now that I
knew about my benefits, I saw that most, if not all, of those flights
would have been free.

I know that as a Christian your major concern is getting from Point A to Point B, like me on a flight. Essentially, most of us became a Christian because we wanted to get safely from Point A (earth) to Point B (eternity in heaven). However, on our way there, God wants us to know there are riches, rights, and privileges we can benefit from as we head to our ultimate destination. It would be a shame to get to heaven only to realize how powerful heaven's authority could have been for you on earth. It would be a shame to get there never having tapped into all you could down here. That's why I, like Paul, want you to be enlightened right now about the kingdom authority you have as well as the benefits and privileges that are yours based on your relationship with Jesus Christ.

A college student had called his mom one day and let her know he was running out of money. He asked her to send him some money so that he would have enough for food until he got back for the break. In a few days, he got a package in the mail from his mom. It wasn't an envelope like he expected. Rather, it was a Bible and a note. The note said, "Son, pray and read your Bible."

The young man called his mom obviously disappointed. "You know I love the Lord, Mom," he said. "But I really need money right now. I'm about to run out."

His mom answered gently, "Son, just pray. And read your Bible." He could almost hear the smile on her face as she said it. But that just caused him to feel more disappointed.

A few days later, he decided to call her again. "Mom," he said. "I'm completely out of money and it's not yet time for spring break."

Much to his frustration, his mom replied exactly how he thought she would. "Son, pray. And read your Bible." This time she sounded more insistent. But he still brushed her off. He didn't know how reading his Bible was going to help him get gas money. Eventually, he got mad. He borrowed some money from a friend and drove home. He was very upset and explained how he had a practical need but she just sent him the Bible. He had even brought the Bible with him as a visual illustration of how un-practically she had answered his request.

"Let me see your Bible," she said. So, the son handed it to her. "Did you read it?" she asked. He nodded his head, although he wasn't telling the truth. His mom then opened the Bible and spread right there in the book of Psalms was five $100 bills. "You didn't read your Bible," she said. "Because if you had prayed and read your Bible, you would have understood there is more in there than you could have ever imagined."

What God wants you to know is that there is more in His Word than you have ever imagined. The Bible isn't just to be held in your hand. It is to be experienced. It is to be put to the test. It is to be lived out and actualized in your everyday life. Paul longed for the Christians at Ephesus to have the eyes of their hearts enlightened because he knew they were wearing fogged-up glasses. It's like trying to wear glasses during the pandemic when everyone was completely masked. If you don't have them on just the right way, they would completely fill with steam and fog, making it nearly impossible to see at all.

Fog on your glasses is like pesticides on your fruit. When you put too many pesticides on your fruit and vegetables, that which was designed and created as organic has now become chemically induced. As a result, it lends itself to the onset of all sorts of potential health problems—even if the taste is somewhat the same as organic. Many of us have put pesticides on what God has for us, and those pesticides have contaminated our spiritual walk. The main pesticide we have applied to our hearts and minds is called human wisdom. Human wisdom is essentially humanity's point of view. The spiritual way to think is God's way to think. God's thoughts are organic. His truth is pure. But when we mess up His thoughts and His truth with human wisdom, we open ourselves to becoming spiritually sick. This happens even though we may spend our time chewing on the Word. Human wisdom always nullifies the manifestation and illumination of the wisdom of God and the kingdom authority He wants us to experience.

Scripture tells us clearly that we already have all we need to live out the fullness of our lives. Ephesians 1:3–4 puts it like this:

> Blessed be the God and Father of our Lord Jesus Christ, who has blessed us with every spiritual blessing in the heavenly places in Christ, just as He chose us in Him before the foundation of the world, that we would be holy and blameless before Him.

Everything God is ever going to do for you He has already done. He has already deposited the spiritual wealth of your inheritance into your account. All you have to do is access it. The story is told of Randolph Hurst, the newspaper tycoon and art collector, who ran across a piece of art in a magazine that really caught his attention. He called up his art dealer to go and find him the original. The art dealer went near and far in search of this special piece of creative genius. After many weeks of searching, he came back to Randolph Hurst empty-handed. "I was unable to locate the original art piece," he said, disappointed to be missing out on his commission no doubt.

But just a few more weeks later, the art dealer was in the basement of Randolph Hurst's home curating some of his art only to discover something unusual. The art piece he had gone to great lengths to locate just weeks before was actually right there in the basement all along. Randolph Hurst already owned it. He just didn't know it or remember that he had it. Many of us are going all over the place looking for answers we already have. We are looking for resources we already have. We are looking for purpose we already have. God wants you to know that what you are looking for is already yours. He has already blessed you with every spiritual blessing in the heavenlies. It's been credited to your account at the finished work of Jesus Christ.

It's hard to remember that sometimes. It's hard to see what is ours sometimes. It's hard to understand the authority at our disposal, especially when we become so consumed with secular thinking and worldly wisdom or our own human emotions and experiences. It's easy to lose sight of the spiritual right before our eyes. That's why Paul wrote what he did. It applied back then just as much as it applies to us today. Paul prayed that the Christians at Ephesus would be able to see "what is the surpassing greatness of His power toward us who believe" (Eph. 1:19). He wanted them, and us, to see God's power. His power is tied to His kingdom authority. Power doesn't amount to much without the authority to use it. Many people who have neglected to pay their electrical bills have power supplied to their homes. They just don't have the authority to have that power supply connected to their main generator because it has been switched off. Power without the authority to use it is useless. Additionally, power is also useless when we fail to flip the switch or plug in the appliances. God won't do for us that which He has commanded us to do in obedience to Him. We must act.

That's why it's critical that you and I come to understand this key to kingdom authority. It is only in accessing the rights and privileges that are ours by virtue of Jesus Christ that we will be able to use it. Otherwise, it just becomes words in a book, similar to my executive Platinum status rewards in my American Airlines book each year, which I never took the time to read or use.

If you are not experiencing God's power in your life, it isn't because God lacks any power. If you are not experiencing God's kingdom authority in your life, it isn't because He lacks any kingdom authority. God's power and authority could be working all around you, but you would never see it when you fail to view life through a spiritual lens. The resurrection power and authority most of us sing about and talk about is only available to us when we access it. God desires to demonstrate His power in your life. He wants you to see Him reverse things, make dead things come alive, turn defeat into victory and take loss and wind up with gain. He wants you to witness Him change the natural order of things, but He will only do that when you see things as they actually are. When you view things spiritually.

The kind of kingdom authority and power God wants us to possess comes through Jesus Christ. We read this as we continue looking at Paul's letter to the church at Ephesus in Ephesians 1:19–23:

> . . . and what is the surpassing greatness of His power toward us who believe. These are in accordance with the working of the strength of His might which He brought about in Christ, when He raised Him from the dead and seated Him at His right hand in the heavenly places, far above all rule and authority and power and dominion, and every name that is named, not only in this age but also in the one to come. And He put all things in subjection under His feet, and gave Him as head over all things to the church, which is His body, the fullness of Him who fills all in all.

Jesus Christ has ultimate kingdom authority because Jesus Christ is seated in a position of authority, above all rule and powers and dominion. His throne is located in heavenly places, which is a euphemism for the spiritual realm. And because Jesus is now seated in the spiritual realm ruling on His throne, His rule overrules everything else beneath Him. Which is, in case you didn't know, *everything*.

To help make sense of this, we can compare it to our political environment today. Decisions are made in Washington, DC. There's the White House, the Capitol, and the Supreme Court. The laws are made by Congress, interpreted by the Supreme Court, and administered by the White House's Executive Branch. All of these three entities work in sync to produce and enforce the laws of the land. In the heavenly realm, we have the Father, the Son, and the Spirit. What the Trinity does is execute and enforce the spiritual and natural laws over all else. And because the Trinity rules over all, God cannot be overruled. His kingdom authority cannot be overturned. Satan cannot deem it unworthy to be enforced. At worst, it just cannot be accessed because His followers fail to understand and apply the rights and privileges due us.

That's why it's critical that the eyes of your heart be opened to the spiritual reality in which we live. You have a wealth of power available to you if you will only discover the key to using it in your own life. When Jesus defeated Satan on the cross, He stripped Satan of any authority over you and me (Heb. 2:14). Satan can no longer defeat us. But because he knows that full well, Satan shifted strategies to try and deceive us into our own personal defeat instead. Now, Satan must trick you to defeat you. He can't overpower you, if you are a believer in Jesus Christ. He has got to dupe you. That's why Satan wants your spiritual eyes to be shut, deeply asleep and oblivious to all God has in store for you. Especially oblivious to the reality that Satan is now a defeated foe underneath Jesus's feet.

The reason why it's important to realize where Jesus sits in the heavenly realm and the kingdom authority that has been vested to Him through His death, resurrection, and ascension is because you sit there too. As a follower of Jesus Christ, you have been raised up to sit with Him in the spiritual realm. Don't just take my word for it either. It's too important a truth for that. Look to the Word, which says,

> But God, being rich in mercy, because of His great love with which He loved us, even when we were dead in our transgressions, made us alive together with Christ (by grace you have been saved), and raised us up with Him, and seated us with Him in the heavenly places in Christ Jesus, so that in the ages to come He might show the surpassing riches of His grace in kindness toward us in Christ Jesus. (Eph. 2:4–7)

The right to use legitimate power within the context of God's will rests in your position with Jesus Christ in the heavenly places. Guess what? Jesus is not the only one in the spiritual realm. You, if you are a follower of Jesus, are there too. I am there too. We're here, but we are also there. We have been relocated spiritually, even though we remain physically on earth right now. The problems take place when we are seated in the heavenly realm but choose to operate from earthly places. We fail to tap into the kingdom authority available to us simply because we choose to function from our position on earth. The reason many of us are not seeing kingdom authority unleashed in our lives is because we are not operating from where the power is. We are operating from a position of lack, in the nasty here and now. As long as you think, function, and live according to human wisdom and human abilities and human power on earth, you will not be tapping into all of the rights and privileges that are yours in the heavenly realm.

If you will learn to view all of life from the perspective of where you are truly seated, which is in the heavenly places, you will begin to see all there is to be seen. If all you see is what you see, then you do not see all there is to be seen. You and I must learn to view all of life from a kingdom focus—a kingdom mindset, an authoritative kingdom perspective. When you learn to operate and make your decisions from where you are truly seated, you will begin to access the authority you need to live out the fullness of your kingdom destiny.

Have you ever noticed when you are in an airplane how small and

> If you will learn to view all of life from the perspective of where you are truly seated, which is in the heavenly places, you will begin to see all there is to be seen.

orderly everything looks down below? That's because you are looking at it from so high up. But when you hit the ground, chaos
ensues because you can no longer see the big picture. Until you
learn to trade in human wisdom for the big picture—divine wisdom—you'll stay stuck in the chaos, mess, and traffic jams of life.
Whether it be personal traffic, familial traffic, circumstantial traffic,
or any other, if you do not learn to view the routes and pathways
of life from the high vantage point of heaven, you will not know
the way to go.

Always start from where you are seated. Face every difficulty,
decision, and drama from where you are seated with Christ in the
heavenlies—above all rule and authority and dominion. Your spiritual connection point to Jesus has placed you high above all else.
Like a Zoom call or teleconferencing video call can take you to
another location, even though you remain physically present where
you are, Jesus has enabled each of us as His followers to function
from the heavenlies, with Him. The problem is that too many of
us have become so used to earth that we never connect the spiritual
technology to heaven, so we wind up with the limitations of earth.
As a result, we fail to actualize the authority and power God has
granted us to experience.

One of the main reasons we fail to actualize our kingdom
authority is because we fail to turn the key. The key is found in two
verses we looked at earlier, Ephesians 1:22–23, which says, "And
He put all things in subjection under His feet, and gave Him as
head over all things to the church, which is His body, the fullness

of Him who fills all in all." Right there is the key. You will not access the kingdom authority available to you unless you are under Jesus's feet. You have to be under His feet, just like everyone and everything else. That means to be under His authority, control, and rule. If you are not under Jesus's rule, you won't get His kingdom authority to act on your behalf. In fact, you can pray until you are blue in the face, but if you are not under His feet through being surrendered to His authority, your prayers will just hit the ceiling and bounce right back.

God only dispenses His kingdom authority from where He sits up on high to benefit us down here when we live underneath the overarching rule of the lordship of Jesus Christ. To put it another way, you and I must settle one issue only. Following salvation, there remains only one overriding issue on the table for every believer in order for them to experience the supernatural work of God in their lives. That is the issue of the *lordship of Jesus Christ over every area of life.* That is the key. That is what must be addressed before you unlock and unleash heaven's authority on your behalf.

When you trust Christ for the forgiveness of sins, you are now on your way to heaven. But when you surrender to the lordship of Jesus

> God only dispenses His kingdom authority from where He sits up on high to benefit us down here when we live underneath the overarching rule of the lordship of Jesus Christ.

Christ over every area of your life, that's when heaven can now visit you on earth. Heaven's power will not come to your aid or relief until you are under the feet of Jesus. That means what He says goes. What He wants goes. What His goals are become your own. Romans 14:7–9 summarizes it great:

> For not one of us lives for himself, and not one dies for himself; for if we live, we live for the Lord, or if we die, we die for the Lord; therefore whether we live or die, we are the Lord's. For to this end Christ died and lived again, that He might be Lord both of the dead and of the living.

Until Jesus is Lord over all—that means Master, Ruler, Final-Decision-Maker—you will not unlock His kingdom authority over that which comes against you. Unless and until you are willing to acknowledge you are not your own but you have been bought with a price (1 Cor. 6:20), then you will be on your own when life's troubles try to trip you up. Jesus is to rule over your personal life, financial life, attitudinal life, relational life, and more. He reigns over it all because He owns it all. After all, He died for it all on the cross. If you want to see Jesus's rule on earth, then you must allow Him to rule you from the heavenlies. This is so because God's philosophy of history is to bring all things under the kingdom rule of Jesus Christ (Eph. 1:10, 22).

One of the issues we face in our culture today is that we have too many AM/FM Christians. They switch frequencies. They are heavenly on Sunday yet then go secular on Monday. They keep switching frequencies back and forth, and then wonder why they don't get to hear the whole song. The reason they don't unlock God's kingdom authority is because God won't let anyone two-time Him. You must decide if He is Lord or if you are. Now, if you are in charge, then that means you must rely on your own maneuvering and manipulation to make it through life. But if Jesus is Lord, then you can rely on His power and authority to overrule that which is in opposition to you living out your purpose and destiny. Unless Jesus is Lord over your thoughts, words, actions, and decisions, He will just become a religious experience to encourage and inspire you. You will never get to see Him come through for you on a level that only He can.

I can tell you firsthand that there is nothing like seeing God show up when you didn't see a way through something you faced. God can flip the natural order of things even when you don't know how He will do it. But He only does that when we surrender to His lordship over all. *Surrender is the key.* It is the passcode. It is the Zoom link. It is the face ID. Surrender is what you need to access the kingdom authority that has been granted to you in the heavenlies.

God is not looking for people to make a commitment to Him. Just like with any New Year's resolution, commitments only last so long. God wants your surrender. When you

> God is not looking for people to make a commitment to Him. Just like with any New Year's resolution, commitments only last so long. God wants your surrender.

surrender, He is in control. He calls the shots. He is the authority. Which, in turn, enables you to unlock His authority in your life for what you need Him to do as well.

CHAPTER TWO

The Conflict

I recently traveled to Ireland to film the teaching sessions for the Bible study book on kingdom authority. We chose Ireland because of its deep history fraught with battles, strife, and struggles to see who would be given the overarching authority to govern the land. In fact, even to this day the nation is divided into Northern Ireland, which is governed by the British, and the remainder of Ireland which is governed by the Irish.

If you were to travel to Northern Ireland, you would be traveling to another country. In fact, you would even need to exchange your euros for pounds if you wanted to gas up your car or go to a restaurant or even buy some souvenirs. The land may appear to be the same land to the average viewer, other than the flags that blow in the wind signifying which nation you are in. But the governing forces of each section of Ireland are distinctly different. As a result, euros are not an accepted currency in Northern Ireland, just as the British pound is not an accepted currency in the remaining parts of the island not governed by the Brits.

The currency reflects a much deeper matter, though. And that is the matter of ownership. It involves the matter of governance. It includes the matter of ultimate allegiance by the citizens and rule by the authorities. While the cows, sheep, and pastures may not differ from one side of the border to the other, the entirety of how things operate and are run as a nation differ significantly.

Visiting Ireland brought this, and many other interesting insights to my perspective. I enjoyed my time in Ireland a lot. Traveling as far west as the Cliffs of Moher to the southern region of Cork, as well as the bustling metropolis of Dublin—I got to meet a number of people who exposed me to a culture steeped in a rich heritage of order and contentment. Rarely have I come across a group of individuals so seemingly content, relaxed, and enjoying themselves with the everyday aspects of life. Ireland presented herself through her citizens as a uniquely kind and friendly place to visit, or live. The pace was much slower as well, allowing for plenty of time to walk, exercise, and enjoy the outdoors. It was refreshing, especially after experiencing the vitriol and violence that has risen to define much of our identity politics in America as well as in our culture at large.

While Ireland is distinctly divided politically between the north and the south, America has begun to experience our own divisions as well. Yet ours are not so specifically established. After all, we continue to be represented politically in one location: Washington, DC. Our nation's capital represents the centerpiece of political power in our land. The three branches of government that oversee the operation of the Constitution among the citizenry of America find their home in DC. Yet even though the location for our nation's leadership lies in one area, the division within our leadership runs deep. Two sides, and sometimes more, conflict with one another on a regular basis. The Democrats and the Republicans clash when it comes to varying worldviews and values.

These divisions give way to personalities within politics who conflict with one another. It opens the floodgate of perspectives, which can at times be as different as night or day. What's worse than the division within our nation's leaders, though, is that it has somehow filtered down and become a division among citizens. The conflict in the House of Congress between the two aisles has turned into a conflict on Main Street America between races, ethnicities, class categories, personalities, and just about any demographic distinction you can name. Never have I seen so much bickering and belittling between those of differing beliefs than I have seen today. It's alarming how far we have fallen. But it isn't surprising when you understand that conflict in leadership leads to discontinuity in those who follow them. The issues in DC create issues in Dallas, Miami, Atlanta, Baltimore, or just about anywhere in our land, depending on the topic at hand.

If there existed unity in our governing leadership, there would also exist greater unity in our citizenry. But, instead, we live as governed recipients—and either active or passive participants—in a political and cultural warfare. You can't say that because you do not live in DC that what happens in DC doesn't matter to you. You will be affected by it whether you acknowledge that reality or not. And if you fail to have an understanding of how Washington works, then you will be somewhat limited in how you should interface with the battles and conflicts that occur beneath the national leadership, in our everyday lives.

The battle in DC is a big one, but a larger conflict looms higher up—the conflict in the spiritual realm itself. There exists a battle for control between God and his enemy, Satan. Satan has made it his goal to usurp the rightful control and governance God has over His creation. As a result, spiritual warfare takes place continually. To the degree that you understand how that conflict works itself out is to the degree you will know how to effectively navigate it. If you fail to understand the complexities of spiritual conflicts, you will relegate yourself to that of an unwitting participant in the deluge of division. Up there always affects down here. Thus, if you and I have conflict down here due to not knowing what's going on up there, then we will always live at a deficit in strategy.

That's why I am glad you've set out with me on this journey to unlock your kingdom authority. It's one of my favorite subjects to study, preach on, write about, and live out. In writing about this concept of kingdom authority, I want to better equip you on how to handle the conflicts down here that are rooted in the cosmic conflict up there—in the spiritual realm. When you can grasp these key aspects of your rightful authority in Christ, you can exercise this authority to your advantage.

Satan has claimed rights over your life and mine. He has filed suit. He has established a plan of action on how to maximize his claims to the fullest while also attempting to erase things out of your destiny—things that are legitimately yours given by God. One of his most effective ways of ruling over you is to get you to fight the wrong enemy. Satan loves to get us caught up in fighting other people—or our family members, spouse, different demographics or groups of people based on identity politics. But when we fall for his schemes, we wind up fighting the wrong war and wrong opponent.

You must always address the root if you want to fix the fruit. You must address the unseen to fix the seen. This is because everything visible and physical is preceded by that which is invisible and spiritual. Everything in the physical realm—what our five senses can perceive—is preceded by that which is unseen to the human eyes. Therefore, if something needs to be addressed, corrected, reclaimed, or restored in the physical realm, you must address the invisible, spiritual reality operating and seeking to rule behind it. If you do not address the invisible and spiritual components, you will fail in your pursuit of overcoming it. That's just how our world works. It's how God established it.

We read in the last chapter that Paul called this spiritual realm the heavenlies. In fact, the Bible tells us in 2 Corinthians that three heavens exist. The first heaven is the Atmospheric Heaven. You and I live in this realm, where there is oxygen, gravity, and the elements we know. The second heaven is the Stellar Heaven. This is the area we identify as housing the stars, sun, and the galaxies. The third heaven is God's Throne Room. This is where God and His angels abide. It is also where Paul visited when he was taken up, as referenced in 2 Corinthians 12:2. It is within this higher spiritual realm that spiritual conflicts take place. And whatever happens in the spiritual trickles down to have an impact in the physical. The spiritual realm is similar to the Washington, DC, of our physical existence. What happens there affects us here.

> You must always address the root if you want to fix the fruit. You must address the unseen to fix the seen. This is because everything visible and physical is preceded by that which is invisible and spiritual.

We read previously in Ephesians 1:3 that all of our blessings lie in these heavenly places. We also saw that Jesus was raised and seated in these heavenly places (vv. 20–21). In Ephesians 2:6, we discovered we have also been raised with Christ in heavenly places, and in 3:10, we discover the church operates in heavenly places. But in Ephesians 6:12, we are introduced to the concept of a war in this space. This passage speaks to the location of the spiritual battles that seek to consume us. We read, "For our struggle is not against flesh and blood, but against the rulers, against the powers, against the world forces of this darkness, against the spiritual forces of wickedness in the heavenly places." The cosmic clash of kingdoms is taking place in the heavenly spiritual realm.

Thus, if you want to address the physical, visible fruit showing up in your everyday thoughts and life, you must first address the invisible, spiritual root located in the spiritual realm. What God has given to you and me during our time on earth is the opportunity to participate in the process of spiritual victory. We participate through understanding and applying the principles of kingdom authority. As a reminder, kingdom authority is *the divinely authorized right and responsibility delegated to believers to act on God's behalf in spiritually ruling over His creation under the lordship of Jesus Christ.*

In Daniel 10, we get a glimpse into a man who is seeking to do just that. He is seeking to use his divinely authorized right to act on God's behalf in spiritually ruling over the problem at hand. He is doing this by fasting and praying about the confusion and chaos around him.

> If you want to address the physical, visible fruit showing up in your everyday thoughts and life, you must first address the invisible, spiritual root located in the spiritual realm.

Later in Daniel's life, he found himself in Persia. It is in Persia where we catch up with him now. It is in Persia where Daniel is praying about the battles raging around him. And it is in Persia where we gain insight into the spiritual world and how it works by examining the results of Daniel's prayer. Let's take a look:

> Then behold, a hand touched me and set me trembling on my hands and knees. He said to me, "O Daniel, man of high esteem, understand the words that I am about to tell you and stand upright, for I have now been sent to you." And when he had spoken this word to me, I stood up trembling. Then he said to me, "Do not be afraid, Daniel, for from the first day that you set your heart on understanding this and on humbling yourself before your God, your words were heard, and I have come in response to your words. But the prince of the kingdom of Persia was withstanding me for twenty-one days; then behold, Michael, one of the chief princes, came to help me, for I had been left there with the kings of Persia. Now I have come to give you an understanding of what will happen to your people in the latter days, for the vision pertains to the days yet future." (vv. 10–14)

One of the most interesting things in this passage has to do with the timing of God's response. It says that on the day Daniel cried out, God responded. But nothing happened on that day in Daniel's world. Daniel still struggled. Daniel still agonized. Even though God responded, there was a delay of twenty-one days before God's response reached Daniel. How can God respond but the response not reach someone for three whole weeks? The answer to that is part of the critical points of our time together in studying this subject of kingdom authority. The reason the answer did not get to Daniel when God responded was because of a prince of Persia who got in the way.

We know who the prince of Persia is because we know who Michael the archangel is. Michael is the lead angel in heaven, which is why he's also called a prince. Thus, if Michael is a prince and he's an angel, then it stands to reason that the prince of Persia is also an angel. But the only angels who would seek to thwart the purposes of God are demons. Demons are those angels who have rebelled against God. Their job is to block heaven's answers to our legitimate prayer requests.

Prayer is an essential requirement for exercising and experiencing kingdom authority. It releases God to do His will on earth. God has both a conditional and unconditional will. His conditional will is what He can only do when we meet His requirements of faith and obedience. His unconditional will is what He sovereignly decides to do independent of our actions. Prayer is God's authorized point of contact for accessing God's conditional will.

You and I have prayer requests hanging up there in the heavenly places, not because God hasn't answered yet but because they have been interfered with and are therefore unreceived. But what you need to know is that you can affect how quickly the response to your prayers reaches you. You have authority when you know how to rightly use it to break the interference that seeks to block God's answers to you.

We learn more about this authority when we look more deeply at the angelic conflict raging all around us. I call it a clash of kingdoms. On one side you have Michael leading an army of angels seeking to carry out God's will in the lives of believers and bring them the answers to their prayers. On the other side, you have the prince of Persia along with an array of demons seeking to block the answers that are due to you and me. Angels fight it out over the various things you and I ask God about.

> Prayer is an essential requirement for exercising and experiencing kingdom authority.

But if you don't know how things work in the spiritual realm and in the clash of kingdoms, then you won't know how to get the answers in the physical realm that you desperately need. As we see by the name of this specific demon who is called the prince of Persia, demons have regions they seek to rule and control. This one was over the lands and people in Persia. Scripture says that every believer has an angel assigned to them (Heb. 1:14). Similarly, every region or every realm has a demon over it. There are demons assigned to hover over individuals, families, communities, churches, and nations. And while there are angels also assigned to fight them, that angel often waits on our participation in the process. We have a participatory role to play in the clash of kingdoms. We are not mere spectators.

To understand this clash of kingdoms more fully, we need to look at Ezekiel 28 (vv. 13 and 17) and Isaiah 14 (vv. 1–12). In these two chapters, we read about how Satan rebelled against God. He established a coup d'état. Satan set himself up as a spiritual Taliban aiming to be "like the Most High." We can interpret that to mean that he wanted to establish his own rival kingdom. Satan didn't want to be under God's kingdom rule. He wanted to be separate. He wanted to be in charge. He wanted others to follow his rules. So, he persuaded one-third of the angels to join him in his rebellion and sought to overtake God and His rule.

But, as you might imagine, it's hard to launch a coup against an omniscient Being. God knew what he was up to, and He cut him off before he could get very far at all. We'll look at this more closely in the next chapter, but for now just know that God found Satan guilty of his rebellion, and He pronounced judgment on him. He prepared hell for him and his fallen angels (Matt. 25:41). In Luke 10:18, we read Jesus proclaim of Satan, "And He said to them, 'I was watching Satan fall from heaven like lightning.'"

Keep in mind, though, Satan didn't fall from heaven to hell. He fell from heaven to earth. Then, he will ultimately fall to hell. Hell is set in a future time for Satan, but He sent Satan to earth for now. Then, God set up His plan to advance His kingdom agenda on earth through cooperation with humanity. God formed humanity as a lesser creature than the angels to demonstrate His power and His glory by showing what He could do through a lesser being (Ps. 8:5).

God chose to create humanity to demonstrate what He could do with a lesser creature who obeyed Him, contrasting with a greater creature who rebelled. You and I were placed on earth to showcase to Satan and his demons the power of God over them.

> God set up His plan to advance His kingdom agenda on earth through cooperation with humanity.

This power is made manifest when we link with God. This is exactly why Satan seeks to destroy or get rid of humanity every chance he can. Seeing as we were put on earth to interfere with the establishment of his rival kingdom, he wants us either out of the way or out of commission as strong warriors for the King.

One way Satan debilitates us from cooperating with God's kingdom agenda is through shifting our focus and allegiance from God to anything else. If and when we choose to operate outside of God's rule, we do not access His authority. God created us with agencies of free will. When we choose to operate underneath His rule, He backs us up. When we don't, He watches us try to handle things on our own.

One of the reasons that many of our prayers are still hung up in space somewhere seemingly stuck to the side of a satellite is because we are not aligning our thoughts, words, and actions under God. Therefore, God is not free to release Michael, or a similar angel to Michael, on our behalf. Anytime there exists a conflict in the seat of power, it interferes with the release and action of that power. A lot of us are being blocked by demons because they have outwitted us in the battle. They have outsmarted us in the clash of kingdoms. They have diverted our attention from what is real and what is true, instead placing it on lies, deception, and all manner of evil. It isn't until we align ourselves under God and His rule, and reach out to Him for His divine assistance, that we access His authority.

When Daniel prayed, he inserted himself into the angelic conflict taking place. Daniel got down on his knees, and he prayed. At the very moment he prayed, God responded. But it wasn't only God who responded. Satan responded as well by sending the prince of Persia to block Daniel's answer to prayer. Prayer is hard for many of us. The reason why it's so hard is because when we pray, we insert ourselves into a cosmic clash of kingdoms. We walk out onto the battlefield. We make ourselves a target.

As long as Satan can keep you from praying, he is satisfied that he has diminished your role in this kingdom battle. But the moment you pray, you usher in the spiritual solutions to the physical problems at hand. You seek to tap into the power that is freely yours by virtue of your relationship with God through Christ Jesus. Because of this, you trigger the enemy, whose chief goal is to make you prayerless. A prayerless Christian is a powerless Christian. Prayer is the point of contact between you and heaven's authority. Like flipping on a switch is the point of contact between the wiring and the light, you must engage the battle to be victorious in the battle.

That is why one of the primary aims of the enemy is to make us prayerless because that means we never turn on the switch, even though the wiring for kingdom authority is in place. Satan will intentionally make prayer difficult to try and dissuade you from doing it. That might come in things that distract you, or sleep that calls to you, or thoughts that overcrowd your mind. Whatever the case, Satan's objective is to reduce the amount of time you and I spend in prayer. Prayer is God's divinely authorized methodology to access heaven's authority for earthly intervention. Prayer is His wiring that connects heaven's authority with humanity's hands and hearts. It is the primary method through which God releases His will on earth.

> A prayerless Christian is a powerless Christian.

In fact, Jesus expressly referred to the church as a "house of prayer." He didn't refer to it as a house of preaching or a house of singing. He called it a house of prayer (Matt. 21:12–13). He does this because prayer is the point of contact. Sermons are not the primary point of contact. Songs are not the primary point of contact. Fellowship is not the primary point of contact. Giving or serving is not the primary point of contact. It is prayer that is our primary point of contact to access God's spiritual authority on earth. Prayer gives us access to God's environment so that He is free to intervene on our behalf in history.

38

Prayer places you in the presence of God so you can have a hearing with the King. And as we saw earlier when we read through the passage in Daniel that set the stage for this chapter, God and His angels view each one of us personally. When the angels looked at Daniel, for example, we see that they saw a man of "high esteem." We read earlier in verse 11 where it says, "He said to me, 'O Daniel, man of high esteem, understand the words that I am about to tell you and stand upright, for I have now been sent to you.'" In other words, the angels and God thought highly of Daniel. Daniel's name came up in conversations. Like a potential buyer seeking to get a home, Daniel had a high credit score. He was a man of high esteem, and that mattered when it came to his prayers being answered.

One of the reasons why Satan can steal so much from us by way of our spiritual authority is because when we pray and God looks at our credit score, He sees that we are not fully committed followers of Jesus. We are just pew warmers on our way to heaven but too busy to do any kingdom-minded work for His glory on earth. When your spiritual credit score is poor, then God knows if He answers your prayers, you'll just waste it more often than not. Daniel had a high spiritual credit score. Thus, when he sought God's intervention, the angel Michael was sent to deflect

> Prayer is God's divinely authorized methodology to access heaven's authority for earthly intervention.

and defeat the prince of Persia so that Daniel could get his answer from the heavenly realms down in the physical reality.

You and I can call in heavenly authority too. It may take some time focusing on rebuilding a spiritual credit score and learning how to pray more consistently, but once you are positioned as a visible and verbal kingdom follower under Christ, you will gain access to greater kingdom authority. If you want to reclaim what the enemy has stolen from you, it is time to start demonstrating to God that you are not His follower just to attend church or check off a box. You are His follower because you want to see His kingdom agenda advanced on earth in such a way that brings glory to Him and good to others. When you do that, you will be well on your way to reclaiming all that the enemy has either blocked or stolen.

CHAPTER THREE

The Courtroom

Have you ever ordered something online only to have it get held up somewhere in the process? You had expected to get it the next day, or even in a few days. But as time moved on and days turned to weeks, you realized that something had gone wrong. At first you may have looked out the window expecting a package to arrive, but as the delay stretched on, you might not have looked in anticipation as much. Especially if the delay lasted several weeks.

We can only imagine what Daniel was feeling when he had prayed to God but not heard any real response in twenty-one days. Did he feel abandoned? Did he feel forgotten? Did he think there might be a glitch in the system called "prayer"? I'm curious if he began to doubt God's interest in him or His willingness to help out. The good thing about Scripture is that we don't have to guess.

41

Daniel 10 gives us insight into how Daniel felt during that time of waiting. We read, "In those days, I, Daniel, had been mourning for three entire weeks. I did not eat any tasty food, nor did meat or wine enter my mouth, nor did I use any ointment at all until the entire three weeks were completed" (vv. 2–3).

Daniel didn't forget about his need or his request only to go about his normal life. The delay in God's reply pushed him into a period of mourning, fasting, and persistent seeking of the Lord. The interesting thing to note, as we saw in the previous chapter, is that God did reply when Daniel prayed initially. It was only that His response got intercepted by demonic forces, causing the agonizing delay Daniel found himself in. Yet because Daniel responded with intentional pursuit rather than apathetic dismissal of his situation, the kingdom authority was actualized and an answer given.

I am sure you and I have prayer requests hanging out there in the heavenly places that are stuck there, not because God has been slow to answer but because His answers have been interfered with by demons. One of the reasons Satan and his minions can steal so much from us in this way is because of our lack of fervency to God and His rule. As I mentioned in the last chapter, the spiritual realm pulls up our spiritual credit score to reveal how much authoritative assistance we are given. If we are not committed to God and His kingdom through how we think, speak, and live but rather are merely a pew warmer, we may not access the full spiritual authority needed to release the answers to our requests.

One of the reasons this is true is because spiritual maturity sheds light on how the blessing or kingdom authority will be used. If you are just going to use it for your own purposes and glory, while ignoring the kingdom of God, then what motivation is there to ensure you get it? If you want to reclaim what the enemy has stolen from you or holds hostage from you, you had better start demonstrating to God that you are not just about going to church if you feel like it. But you have to demonstrate through how you live that you are here to be a verbal, visible follower of Jesus Christ. God has all you need to fully live out your destiny, but He will not release the kingdom authority necessary to access it until He sees you are serious about His rule and His glory.

We may think that we are taking care of ourselves by focusing more on ourselves than on God and His kingdom. But in reality, we are short-changing ourselves. We are cheating ourselves. We do this by leaving the spiritual doors unlocked and the windows wide open so Satan can steal from what God has provided for us in the heavenlies. As a result, far too many of us are living under this cloud of spiritual theft, unfortunately enabled through our own personal choices. We have given Satan the opportunity to sneak in to steal our joy. He has stolen our relationships. He has swiped our mental and emotional well-being. He has even stolen our progress in life. But worst of all, Satan has stolen our hope.

When you and I look around at the world in which we live, it is easy to spend a large part of our time giving cultural, social, political, racial, and economic analysis of why things are the way they are. We come up with all sorts of sociological explanations for what has gone wrong. Yet what I am seeking to reinforce in my teaching and through this book is the reality that everything we become entangled with or experience in the visible and physical world is preceded by that which is invisible and spiritual.

In order to address and correct the visible and physical reality in which we live, we must identify the invisible and spiritual cause. Only by identifying and addressing the invisible and spiritual cause can we address the root behind what we see manifesting around us. As I've said before, if all you see is what you see, you do not see all there is to be seen. If you only function in the physical realm of the five senses, then the enemy will be able to rip you off.

For you to identify and reclaim what is rightfully yours, as well as to ascertain all God has planned for you, you must understand and enact God's perspective related to kingdom authority. There's one phrase in Scripture that if you were to ever truly grasp its meaning and truth, you would open a floodgate of spiritual opportunity and authority all around you. It is found in Daniel 4:26 and it appears in Daniel's interpretation of the vision for King Nebuchadnezzar. It says, "And in that it was commanded to leave the stump with the roots of the tree, your kingdom will be assured to you after you recognize that it is Heaven that rules."

For King Nebuchadnezzar to actualize the fullness of the kingdom granted to him, he had to understand one key truth. It is the same key truth we need to recognize and apply as well: *heaven rules*. It is heaven that rules over all. Heaven not only rules the realms of the heavenlies but also the physical realm in which we live. Thus, whatever is breaking down in our lives in the physical realm has emanated from another realm that rules over it.

I love the way Psalm 103:19 puts it when it talks of God's sovereign rule. We read, "The LORD has established His throne in the heavens, and His sovereignty rules over all." God is in charge, even when things are in disarray. When you understand that He has the ultimate say over all, it changes your priorities. When you recognize who sits on the throne above all politicians, celebrities, influencers, billionaires, and the like, it changes who you spend your time listening to, following, and seeking to align with.

Daniel describes God's position in the heavenlies over all when we read about a vision in Daniel 7:9–10:

> "I kept looking
> Until thrones were set up,
> And the Ancient of Days took His seat;
> His vesture was like white snow
> And the hair of His head like pure wool.
> His throne was ablaze with flames,
> Its wheels were a burning fire.
> A river of fire was flowing
> And coming out from before Him;
> Thousands upon thousands were attending Him,
> And myriads upon myriads were standing before
>   Him;
> The court sat,
> And the books were opened."

A throne is where a king rules. As we see in this vision, God is sitting on His throne ruling over all. But we also see something distinct in the passage that if you miss it, it will leave out an important part of kingdom authority. We read that the court sat and the books were opened before God. This is a throne in a courtroom. The ruler in a courtroom is a judge. God is not only King, but He is also Judge who renders legal verdicts and decrees coming from His throne. For you to understand how the world works and how it affects your life, you must not only understand the rule of God, but you also must understand the judgments of God. He is both Ruler and Judge. When God renders judgments in His courtroom, they are always righteous judgments because He is the righteous and sovereign King.

If you have ever been to court or have witnessed a court proceeding on television, you know the decision of the judge can change a life for good or for bad. The judge carries a lot of weight. The same is true for how we live in our everyday lives. God's decisions carry a lot of weight. What He determines for us can change our lives for good or for bad. That is why it is critical we learn first that we are in a courtroom where God is the Judge, and second, we learn how to carry ourselves in this courtroom called life.

If we read a little further down in Daniel 7, we get a greater look into how God rules as Judge. This passage presents a future picture of the anti-Christ, who is going to seek to usurp God's rule. But it also shows up that the anti-Christ will be brought to court and that when he is brought to court, the sovereignty and dominion of God will override him. These verses talk directly about what we call the "end times," the three and a half years that the anti-Christ seeks to subvert the saints and the program of God. And it offers us assurance of God's ultimate victory over the chaos Satan stirs up. We read this in verses 25–27:

> "'He will speak out against the Most High and wear down the saints of the Highest One, and he will intend to make alterations in times and in law; and they will be given into his hand for a time, times, and half a time. But the court will sit for judgment, and his dominion will be taken away, annihilated and destroyed forever. Then the sovereignty, the dominion and the greatness of all the kingdoms under the whole heaven will be given to the people of the saints of the Highest One; His kingdom will be an everlasting kingdom, and all the dominions will serve and obey Him.'"

God is the King sitting on the throne able to also act as Judge over all. Even Satan will come under His judgment. It is God's kingdom that is an everlasting kingdom. He is the One in charge. And even if Satan seeks to rob you or cancel you by accusing you (Rev. 12:10), God has the final say. God rules over all. But, keep in mind, in order to avail ourselves of His rule, you and I must cooperate with His kingdom agenda so we can tap into His kingdom authority. They go hand in hand.

When you read your Bible, you will find a great deal of legalese in it. You'll discover judges, judgments, laws, and even lawsuits.

This should not be surprising since God operates His kingdom in a legal fashion. His is a legal governance, often known as covenants, which apply to the various aspects of life. The goal of God's legal program is to institute His plan. But the goal of Satan is to take you to court, accuse you, and appeal to the Judge as to why you should not get access to the fulfillment of God's good plan. He takes you and me to court to argue why we do not deserve that answer to prayer we desire. He argues why we should not get that deliverance from the dilemma that is consuming us. Or why we should not feel the relief from the financial burden upon us. Or even why we should not get a reversal of the situation in which we are bound. Satan both charges and accuses the spiritual followers of Jesus Christ every moment of every day. Which is why what you think, say, and do matters. Aligning your life under God's overarching rule is a key part to unlocking your kingdom authority.

If you'll recall in the passage we read as I opened this chapter, we saw that in the courtroom and throne room of God, "the books were opened." If we want to know what is in the books, we need to look elsewhere in Scripture. Psalm 139:16 gives us a glimpse. We read, "Your eyes have seen my unformed substance; and in Your book were all written the days that were ordained for me, when as yet there was not one of them." Each of our days have been ordained for us, written down in the book. We all have a book. Your book is what God has written down for you from even before you were born. It's His purpose, plan, and destiny for you.

The goal of our books is revealed to us in Hebrews 10:5–7:

> Therefore, when He comes into the world, He says,
> "Sacrifice and offering You have not desired,
> But a body You have prepared for Me;
> In whole burnt offerings and sacrifices for sin
> You have taken no pleasure.
> Then I said, 'Behold, I have come
> (In the scroll of the book it is written of Me)
> To do Your will, O God.'"

This passage is Jesus talking about when He came into bodily form on earth. His life was lined out in the contents of the book, and that involved the prime objective, which was to "do Your will, O God." Jesus is our guide. He is the One we follow. Thus, just like in His book, our book also has a prime objective, which is to do the will of God. It has our purpose and our plan in it, but just because it has been written down does not mean it will automatically be lived out. We are creatures of divinely bestowed free will. This is why Satan sought to tempt Jesus in the wilderness and get him off track by causing Him to disobey the Word of God. When that didn't work, he tried another plan and that was to cut His life short. But even as Jesus anguished in the garden of Gethsemane, He stayed with His book, "not what I will, but what You will" (Mark 14:36).

Satan spent all of his time seeking to take Jesus away from the plan God purposed for Him, but even after death, Jesus defeated Satan's plan by rising again. The goal of Satan is no different for you and me who follow Jesus and represent His kingdom rule on earth.

Satan wants to take away from our lives the purpose for which we were created in the first place. The further he can get you or me off-track, the more successful he is at accomplishing his goal. Satan is relentless. He will seek to trip us up, accuse us, distract us, lull us to sleep, delight us into disobedience—any number of things. Yet despite his many tactics and methods, his goal remains the same—to strip us of our legal right to accessing the full kingdom authority God has available to us. When he does that, he simultaneously reduces the advancement of God's kingdom agenda on earth through His followers.

There exists a biblical term for our legal connection with God. It's found throughout the book of Daniel, but it's also found throughout the Bible. It's the word *covenant*. When God was giving His law as recorded for us in the book of Exodus, He was telling how a nation ought to run, and how a nation's laws should be executed. In the midst of giving this law, we read about the covenant:

> "'Now then, if you will indeed obey My voice and keep My covenant, then you shall be My own possession among all the peoples, for all the earth is Mine; and you shall be to Me a kingdom of priests and a holy nation.' These are the words that you shall speak to the sons of Israel." (Exod. 19:5–6)

In this passage, we are introduced to the concept of the covenant. If you've heard me preach or read any of my books, you may already be familiar with this term. The covenant is a central theme to the kingdom agenda, which I have focused on heavily over the past four decades. As a reminder, I define the kingdom agenda *as the visible manifestation of the comprehensive rule of God over every area of life.* A covenant fits within the schematic of how God operates His kingdom rule.

A covenant can be defined as *a divinely created relational bond through which God orchestrates His rule, inclusive of blessings and consequences.* God runs His kingdom covenantally. What this means in everyday language is that He has established rules that are spiritually and legally binding by which He has set things up to operate.

For example, the United States has a covenantal document. It's called the Constitution. This covenantal document overlays the definition of the nation. That means when you go to court, and most particularly to the Supreme Court, the job of those making decisions is to interpret whatever it is you are going through or addressing through the lens of the Constitution. The Constitution is to serve as the ruling document over all. Court-authorized decisions, when done right, fall underneath the covenantal covering of the Constitution. If they don't, they can be re-tried as unconstitutional and ultimately overturned.

Similarly, God has a covenant. He has a divinely created bond. All of our lives are to operate according to His covenant. When we align ourselves beneath His clearly outlined rule, we will experience and access the kingdom authority that is ours by right of His covenant. When we don't, we won't. Covenantal alignment is imperative for the exercise of kingdom authority. It was this alignment that gave David victory over Goliath (1 Sam. 17:26, 36). And it is the same alignment that will give us authority to deal with the mammoth challenges in our lives.

One of the key aspects of a covenant is "sanctions." These are the blessings and the curses that are tied to behavioral choices. We read about this in Deuteronomy 28, where God clearly lays out both the blessings and the curses that come attached to the Israelites' choices. This is also true for believers today (1 Cor. 10:16–22; 11:23–32). As a reminder, we have all been given free will. We are free to choose what we think, say, and do. But underneath God's overarching, covenantal rule, we are not free to choose the consequences of our choices. Those have been previously established.

For example, at a red light there is nothing physically preventing you from running the red light. You are free to go through it if you choose. But there does exist a law that says if you run the red light, you are liable for the consequences. These consequences could range from a ticket for running a red light clear up to being held culpable if anyone was injured when you ran the red light. God has given all of us free will. He doesn't send His angels to prevent us from doing the things He doesn't want us to do. But what He does make clear is that if and when we choose to live apart from alignment under His rule, we will also be choosing the consequences and curses that result from our disobedience.

Covenants are legally binding agreements. They are not about how you feel. Just like when a couple gets married, they may marry on feelings, but the legal agreement they enter into remains in place even in those times they don't really feel like it at all. A covenant is a divinely created relational bond. It's more than a contract, like when you sell or buy a house, and more than an agreement. A contract is usually based on shared mutual interests, but a covenant demands a relationship. It is tied to the relationship. In fact, the relationship is part of the covenant.

You'll recall in the previous chapter we read that Daniel was a man of "high esteem." The angel Michael approached him and let him know he was held highly in the heavenly realm. This so-called spiritual "clout" enabled Daniel to effectively pray through the interception that Satan had put in place blocking the answer to his prayer. Daniel positioned himself in this arena of "high esteem" by consistently modeling a kingdom life in a secular land. He remained faithful to God through the highs and the lows. As a result, his prayers carried more weight and authority.

In the legal terms in our nation, to have the "high esteem" to be heard in court is what we call "standing." The court has to determine whether or not the case and those bringing the case are worthy to be heard and fall within the legal parameters of their purview. There exist all kinds of cases that come before the Supreme Court and they can't hear them all, so what must first be examined is this issue of "standing." A lot of people are calling on heaven to hear them and they are praying to God to get results, but God is looking at whether or not there is "standing." He wants to know if there is a legitimate basis for laying claim to God for the case.

Knowing this, Satan will often spend his time accusing the followers of Christ. He is attempting to strip us of our standing. He doesn't want our prayers or requests to reach the throne room of God in a way that allows them to be enacted upon. So he seeks to trip us up in any which way he can and then accuse us that we do not have spiritual standing. That's why it is critical to position yourself in how you live so that when you need God to have your back, He does. Or when you seek to reclaim what the enemy has stolen, God intervenes for you. You and I establish standing by pursuing an authentic, committed relationship with the Lord.

Everybody wants God to rule on their behalf. Everybody wants to be highly favored. Everybody wants God to do something for them. But not everybody is pursuing a relationship with Him. In fact, most people have little time for God. They have little interest in His Word. They don't care to include Him and His perspective in their thoughts and decisions. But then when they need something from Him, they run to Him and ask, only to say He doesn't care when the response gets intercepted in the heavenly realm by the accuser, Satan.

If you are tired of being robbed of your spiritual authority and of that which is legitimately yours as recorded in your book—God's will for your life—then seek God. Pursue a relationship with Him. Learn His Word and align your thoughts, heart, words, and actions underneath it. Satan's goal is to take you down. His goal is to shut you down before you ever achieve your divine destiny. But you can overcome the enemy and his attacks by understanding how to access your legal kingdom authority. It's not about just saying a prayer. It's about what covenantal relational standing is behind that prayer. Some people pray all day but don't have the relational connection to God to give weight to what they say. God doesn't just hear your words; He examines your heart. He looks at your life. He takes into account more than just this moment in time because He values a relationship with you, which demonstrates that you honor His rightful place over all.

Can you imagine what would have happened if a peasant went to a king in a faraway land centuries ago and asked for a parcel of land and all the provisions he needed to farm it? The request would have been ignored because that's not how it works with rulers and rules. But if the same peasant had a relationship with the king—served him and honored him—the king may have heard his request in a whole new way.

> God doesn't just hear your words; He examines your heart. He looks at your life.

Thankfully, God is not a human king given to whims or emotions. He has clearly established rules in His covenantal design that allows us to know what we need to do to access His provisions of blessing and His kingdom authority from the courtroom of heaven. He hasn't hidden any of this from us. It is up to each of us to invest the time, heart, and mind so we get to know God's ways and His will, discovering the power of divine authority released within and through us as we live out our days. That's something I hope to help you with as we continue to explore this topic together.

CHAPTER FOUR

The Verdict

It's clear that God rules from the heavens and His rule is based in an established set of spiritual laws. To understand kingdom authority in the context of the courtroom and all that it entails is an accurate way of examining it. We are familiar with courtrooms, even if we have never been in one ourselves. This is because their story lines often dominate television or movie plots. As well, a number of court cases and trials have dominated the news airwaves and social media feeds over the last few years. People stay glued to their sets watching the various trials and hoping the verdict will go the way they feel it should. Protestors often line the streets or gather outside of courthouses to either cheer or bemoan a verdict.

But there is another verdict that most people long for even more than whatever the current trial is. It's a verdict relating to ourselves. This is because many of us live underneath the weight of the guilt and the shame of our sins.

Many believers need to hear a verdict of "not guilty" to relieve us from the guilt of the accusations against us. We know what we have done. We know the sins we have committed. We know the pain we have caused, not only to others but also to ourselves—and most importantly, to God. We know what it is to need the mercy of the court. We understand how it feels to stand before the One in authority and hope for a release from the guilt and the consequences because the verdict will impact your destiny.

A verdict of guilty sends a person to prison. A verdict of not guilty allows the person to resume his or her life and pursue their purpose.

What takes place when a verdict gets handed down is never just about that moment in time. It always involves the future. The verdict speaks into what will, or will not, be possible to take place in the future.

That is why it is so critical to understand your position and identity in Jesus Christ. Satan has taken up a case against you. What's more, if we were to be authentic and honest, he has just cause for his case. You, like every other human being, have done things that are wrong. You, and I, have sinned. But Jesus Christ stands as our Defense Attorney if and when you know Jesus Christ as your Savior. He represents each of us as His followers in the courtroom of heaven.

When a football team fumbles the football and the other team recovers the ball, a major shift has occurred. A major shift has taken place because the team that was on the offense is now on the defense. The team that was on the defense is now on the offense due to the fumble. God put Adam in the offensive position to rule the earth when He created him. But Adam fumbled the ball. As a result, Satan and his demons picked up the fumble and changed the trajectory of history. First John 5:19 says, "We know that we are of God, and that the whole world lies in the power of the evil one."

Thus, while God is the Creator of the world, humanity handed it over to the demonic realm because Adam fumbled the ball. And the reality is that most of us continue to fumble the ball like Adam. We continue to yield legal rights that belong to us over to the enemy. Satan ends up with a lot of control simply because our sinful choices have given him that control.

That's why it is so critical to understand the verdict gained for each of us at Calvary. Paul writes about this verdict in his letter to the church at Colossae. He wants them to understand the truth of their victory and the reality of their freedom. Because Satan operates in an ongoing strategy against believers each day, we must realize and apply the power of Christ's work in our lives.

Colossians 1:13–14 sets this stage for us when it says, "For He rescued us from the domain of darkness, and transferred us to the kingdom of His beloved Son, in whom we have redemption, the forgiveness of sins." When you accepted Jesus Christ as your Savior, you were transferred to another realm and another kingdom. We will dive deeper into this other realm in the next chapter, but for now I want you to know that this other realm comes with its own terms. In this new kingdom, you and I live underneath God's divine authority. It is His rulership carried out through His Son Jesus Christ that dictates all.

Thus, in order for Satan to rule over you in this new kingdom—he has to get you out from underneath God's rightful and legitimate authority. He has to deceive you in believing you still reside in his kingdom of darkness, or he has to tempt you to rebel against God. In rebelling, you forsake where you have been placed in the kingdom of light and you go back to operate where you had once been transferred from. Satan cannot take away your salvation. But what he can do is ruin your destiny. He can't mess with your status in heaven and eternity, but he can tear up your life on earth. Yet to do this, he has to lure you back out of that protective covering you now have in this new kingdom of light.

> When you accepted Jesus Christ as your Savior, you were transferred to another realm and another kingdom.

One of the primary ways Satan does this is through the power of lies. We read about this in Colossians 2:8–10:

> See to it that no one takes you captive through philosophy and empty deception, according to the tradition of men, according to the elementary principles of the world,

rather than according to Christ. For in Him all the fullness of Deity dwells in bodily form, and in Him you have been made complete, and He is the head over all rule and authority . . .

Essentially, these verses remind each of us to stop being duped. They remind us to wise up to Satan's tricks and deceptions. When we buy into the stories he tells, he gains the upper hand over our lives and our well-being.

Many of you reading this book studied philosophy in college. I describe philosophy as basically doodling with ideas. It involves human thought about the meaning of life, which more often than not resorts to educated guesswork. But when Paul wrote this letter to the church at Colossae, he did so to warn them, and us, to stop being duped by philosophy. Philosophy is often comprised of a worldly perspective. It involves a worldview rooted in human reasoning. It can take many forms such as political philosophy, scientific philosophy, and environmental philosophy. It's basically man's thinking that, more often than not, disagrees with Christ. Paul calls these traditions of men "elementary principles."

It's interesting that he refers to these worldviews as "elementary." It doesn't matter what your degree is or how long you have studied. Whenever you listen to humanity's viewpoint over and above God's, you have reduced yourself to kindergarten-level thinking. You've played the child's game Chutes and Ladders and landed on a chute, thus sending yourself all the way back to elementary school. Unfortunately, we have a lot of elementary school Christians who hang their hats on whatever the current popular thought or trend may be.

Paul instructs us how to be free from these damaging philosophies. He lets us know first and foremost that the wisdom of this world is foolishness, as we read in 1 Corinthians 1:18–21:

> For the word of the cross is foolishness to those who are perishing, but to us who are being saved it is the power of God. For it is written,
>
> > "I will destroy the wisdom of the wise,
> > And the cleverness of the clever I will set aside."
>
> Where is the wise man? Where is the scribe? Where is the debater of this age? Has not God made foolish the wisdom of the world? For since in the wisdom of God the world through its wisdom did not come to know God, God was well-pleased through the foolishness of the message preached to save those who believe.

Paul later goes on to tell us how not to yield to the foolishness of this world when he tells us later in 2 Corinthians 10:5, "We are destroying speculations and every lofty thing raised up against the knowledge of God, and we are taking every thought captive to the obedience of Christ." It is through taking each of our thoughts captive to the truth of Christ that we identify what is true and what is a lie. God wants your mind to be focused on Jesus Christ so much that Jesus becomes the filter through which everything else flows.

Every thought. Every idea. Every ideology. Every political nuance. Every economic philosophy. Every social strategy. Everything that comes to your mind needs to be sifted by Jesus to such a degree that deception is removed entirely. Jesus is the sum of all knowledge. If and when you operate off of anything outside of the truth of Christ, you are operating in a thought form of worldly wisdom. That's when Satan can have his way with you or with any believer who abides in earthly philosophy rather than eternal truth. Satan has his hand in controlling this world order. Be mindful not to adopt a mentality that has been designed to ensnare you, but rather adopt the mind of Christ.

It is in Christ that all fullness of deity dwells (Col. 2:9). We see the power that Jesus holds when we look at what Paul penned in Colossians 1:15–22. It says,

> He is the image of the invisible God, the firstborn of all creation. For by Him all things were created, both in the heavens and on earth, visible and invisible, whether thrones or dominions or rulers or authorities—all things have been created through Him and for Him. He is before all things, and in Him all things hold together. He is also head of the body, the church; and He is the beginning, the firstborn from the dead, so that He Himself will come to have first place in everything. For it was the Father's good pleasure for all the fullness to dwell in Him, and through Him to reconcile all things to Himself, having made peace through

the blood of His cross; through Him, I say, whether things on earth or things in heaven.

And although you were formerly alienated and hostile in mind, engaged in evil deeds, yet He has now reconciled you in His fleshly body through death, in order to present you before Him holy and blameless and beyond reproach . . .

The reason why we are to listen to Jesus is because all the fullness of deity dwells in Him. He knows more than everyone else. All that makes God who God is, is resident in Jesus Christ. That's why Jesus is to have first place in everything. There exists no subject, no system, and no circumstance where Jesus does not rightfully deserve to be the decision-maker. In fact, your first question on every subject ought to be: *What does Jesus think or say about this?* That should be the perspective by which you operate your life. According to Hebrews 2:7–8, everything has been placed underneath Jesus's feet. If we return to the book of Colossians and look at chapter 2, we can see how every single thing is connected to Jesus. This is revealed to us through the words "in Him," which we read repeatedly in verses 9–11:

> For *in Him* all the fullness of Deity dwells in bodily form, and *in Him* you have been made complete, and He is the head over all rule and authority; and *in Him* you were also circumcised with a circumcision made without hands, in

the removal of the body of the flesh by the circumcision of Christ. (emphasis added)

We are to be identified with Jesus in all things since all things are *in Him*. Jesus is to be our point of reference. If something doesn't align with Him, then it ought not to have a place in your thoughts or decisions. One way you can identify what aligns with Jesus is through testing it against the truth of God's Word. First John 4 tells us,

> Beloved, do not believe every spirit, but test the spirits to see whether they are from God, because many false prophets have gone out into the world. By this you know the Spirit of God: every spirit that confesses that Jesus Christ has come in the flesh is from God; and every spirit that does not confess Jesus is not from God; this is the spirit of the antichrist, of which you have heard that it is coming, and now it is already in the world. You are from God, little children, and have overcome them; because greater is He who is in you than he who is in the world. (vv. 1–4)

We are to test each spirit and every thought based on whether or not it aligns with Jesus Christ. Keep in mind, spirits will often do their bidding through a human form. That's what gives rise to false prophets and the like. Anyone who makes the world their basis for right or wrong is yielding to the evil spiritual influence of Satan. First John 4:5 puts it like this: "They are from the world;

therefore they speak as from the world, and the world listens to them." Worldly wisdom is evil wisdom. It is not from Christ.

But those of us who wish to tap into the spiritual authority of God's kingdom are not to align our thoughts with the world. We are to align our thoughts with the truth of Christ so we can test that which is false. First John 4:6 states, "We are from God; he who knows God listens to us; he who is not from God does not listen to us. By this we know the spirit of truth and the spirit of error."

The way we know what we are hearing or reading is true is that it aligns with the truth of God in Christ. Jesus has something to say on every situation we go through. He came in the flesh to identify with the various circumstances we face on earth. He came in the flesh because He wants to speak into our choices and decisions. He has something to say about your human existence because He is not only God up high in heaven, but He is also human down here on earth. He wants to speak into your relationships. He wants to speak into your financial choices. He wants to speak into politics. He wants to speak into social scenarios and culture wars. He wants to speak into your emotional well-being and healing. Most importantly, He wants to speak into your position before God in the heavenly realm. He wants to declare you "not guilty" where Satan stands before you, accusing you of guilt.

Returning to Colossians 2 where we looked at everything being found "in Christ," we see then that when we choose to identify our thoughts, words, actions, and lives with Jesus Christ—we receive the benefit of His authority. We read this in the next verses,

Having been buried with Him in baptism, in which you were also raised up with Him through faith in the working of God, who raised Him from the dead. When you were dead in your transgressions and the uncircumcision of your flesh, He made you alive together with Him, having forgiven us all our transgressions, having canceled out the certificate of debt consisting of decrees against us, which was hostile to us; and He has taken it out of the way, having nailed it to the cross. (vv. 12–14)

All of this is legal language. The decrees are legal accusations. Satan comes against believers from a legal standpoint, holding our sins and prior thoughts, words, and actions against us. Since Satan can't remove a believer's salvation, he will try everything he can to get a believer from experiencing all there is to experience in the spiritual realm. He uses God's perfect, divine nature to point out how sinful we are as humans and state that we do not deserve nor can we have fellowship with a holy God. Due to our sin, Satan argues that God cannot answer our prayers nor give us breakthroughs, peace, or even joy. Satan holds these decrees against us.

But what we must keep in mind is that Jesus Christ has "canceled out the certificate of debt consisting of decrees against us" (Col. 2:14). Jesus has canceled it. He has voided it. He has removed the debt that sin stacked up in our accounts. He has made it possible for each of us to live free from the legal debt of our own sins.

One of the reasons people fail to pay off financial debt is due to interest rates. They may make minimal payments on the debt, but as they do, the interest continues to accumulate. It becomes a vicious cycle of slavery to debt repayment. In the spiritual realm, Satan wants to keep us stuck in a loop where he adds interest to our sin debt and we have to try to keep digging out of the guilt, shame, and consequences that sin brings to bear. When we are stuck in this loop, we are prevented from living out the kingdom purpose for which God created us.

And while God will never lower His standard or lessen His own holiness, He has provided a way for us to be free from sin's debt and Satan's accusation. This way is through the finished work of Jesus Christ. That's why when we read the word *tetelestai* in John 19:30, we see that Jesus used a legal term to declare that the work He had come to do was "finished." The term literally means, "paid in full." On the cross, Jesus paid for your sin through His substitutionary atonement. Jesus paid the penalty that you owed to a Holy God so that when Satan brings the legitimate accusations of sinfulness against you, God can declare you "not guilty" by virtue of the legal payment of Jesus Christ. The cross of Christ represented the greatest legal transaction in history.

Second Corinthians 5:21 puts it like this: "He made Him who knew

> Jesus paid the penalty that you owed to a Holy God so that when Satan brings the legitimate accusations of sinfulness against you, God can declare you "not guilty" by virtue of the legal payment of Jesus Christ.

no sin to be sin on our behalf, so that we might become the righteousness of God in Him." We call this the substitutionary atonement. This is where Jesus took what you and I owed to God, and Jesus picked up the tab Himself. Not only did He pick up the tab to make the payment, but He also transferred His perfect credit score (His righteousness) to us. This great legal transaction took place on the cross because God cannot change His standard of holiness. The wrath of God comes against all sin. But Jesus, in His great compassion, took that wrath on our behalf.

What's more, following this legal transaction, He also implemented new rules for the evil regime. In fact, He disarmed them. We read in Colossians 2:15–17,

> When He had disarmed the rulers and authorities, He made a public display of them, having triumphed over them through Him.
>
> Therefore no one is to act as your judge in regard to food or drink or in respect to a festival or a new moon or a Sabbath day—things which are a mere shadow of what is to come; but the substance belongs to Christ.

What Jesus did in forgiving our sins is strip away the weapons of the rulers and authorities in Satan's realm. He disarmed them. He took the bullets out of the devil's gun. He removed their firepower. As Jesus did that, He set you free from your past but also in your present. All you need to do to fully maximize the life He's created you to live and experience the full kingdom authority that is yours is align your heart, mind, and actions with Jesus. Satan has no legitimate weapons to use against you. His only trick now is deception. If Satan can get you out from under the authoritative covering of the truth of God's Word, he can strip you of your freedom. But as long as you remain under Christ and His Word, you will be free.

What God made legal in the death of Jesus Christ, you make literal through your public confession of Christ. The legal has been achieved. But the literal must be accessed. God has done up there in the heavenly realm what only your public confession of Christ can bring into existence down here on earth. Thus, if you are ashamed of Christ or if worldly philosophy overrules Christ's Word, then you've joined your own prosecution. You've joined the devil's side. You've joined their verdict, which is based on deception. The way to live free of the guilt of sin is through your public identification with the death, burial, and resurrection of Jesus Christ.

There's a story told that during the Civil War a man named Pratt paid a man named White to go to war and be his substitute. The man who went to war for him wound up dying in the war. Shortly after that, the government drafted Pratt again. But Pratt went to the Draft Board and told them they could not draft him. The reason being was that the substitute who went to war for him had died. He successfully argued, that if his substitute died in his place, then he should also be considered legally dead, and anyone who is legally dead could not be drafted for a war. In the courtroom, you might call that "double jeopardy." This means that you cannot try someone for the same thing again once they've been declared innocent.

Since Jesus Christ has declared His followers who trust in Him as innocent (justification means to be legally acquitted), the devil cannot pull a double jeopardy on any of us. We are covered by the blood of Christ. This is the truth. The only way Satan can get you living a life of guilt, shame, and pain due to sin's consequences is in deceiving you into believing you were never declared innocent to begin with. But he who the Son sets free, is free indeed (John 8:31–32, 36). The verdict against you, and the verdict against me—thanks to Calvary—is: Not Guilty. As we go through these next few pages together, we'll explore how to maximize that verdict in your everyday life, primarily through your repentance of sin and worship of Christ and submission to Christ and His Word.

CHAPTER FIVE

The Realm

 Many, if not most of you will remember the name Thomas Anderson. He also went by the name, Neo, in the film *The Matrix*. Thomas Anderson was a computer programmer and part-time computer hacker who lived a regular, plain, ordinary working day life. He exemplified the everyday man—doing the best he could with what he had. That is, until one day when he was given the understanding that he was actually in a computer-generated reality called the matrix.

When Anderson became aware of this new realm, he ran into things that blew his mind. He ran into powers he didn't know he had. He ran into a new relationship that he hadn't even dreamed of having before. He ran into an entirely new community of people in a place he had never known before—a place called Zion. But along with all of the good Neo found, he also ran into something—or someone—very bad. He ran into an enemy named Mr. Smith.

In the first film about his experiences, there took place an insightful dialogue between Neo and a character named Morpheus. In that discussion, Morpheus told him they'd been waiting for him to arrive. They had waited for this man who would come from another realm and transition into what Morpheus called "the real world." They had been waiting for him to defeat Mr. Smith so they could all live free of his evil control.

In this conversation, Morpheus explained to Neo that the world he had come from was not the real world. He explained what happened there was not reality. Rather, Morpheus shared that where Neo was with him right then—inside of the matrix—was what was real. In fact, it was so real that what happened in the matrix affected what happened in the world from which he had come. There existed this unseen realm that influenced the seen and known realm of his previous experience.

The next part of the dialogue most people will recognize, even if you've never seen the movie at all. That's when Morpheus offered Thomas Anderson a choice of two pills. He told him he could take the "blue pill" and then go back to his ordinary life, or he could take the "red pill" if he wanted to enter the realm of what was real. The question boiled down to whether or not he wanted to choose the predictable and plain or whether or not he wanted to experience the extraordinary and supernatural behind it all.

This movie series always stuck with me because it really does give an illustration of a choice that is actually laid out before us all. Many of us have settled for plain and ordinary lives within the known, physical realm of our five senses. We have settled for the regular routines while disregarding the supernatural that steers everything from beyond. In fact, far too many people have settled for just trying to get by and just trying to make it, eking out an existence. In this daily grind, they have even forgotten how to aim high or to dream big or live with any amount of personal and spiritual authority any longer. They just want to get through today so they can get through this week so they can do it all over again come Monday.

The reason why so many have settled for this may be because many have gotten used to functioning in the wrong realm. They have identified with the wrong environment. They have mistakenly believed this world of the five senses is the real world when, in all actuality, the spiritual realm is far more real than we could ever comprehend. Yet, for a person to fully maximize his or her potential by living with kingdom authority, he or she must recognize the underlying influence for all that takes place in the here and now. They must recognize the supernatural reality that connects, moves, and motivates all that occurs in the natural world known as our earth.

The writer of Hebrews takes us to this place of supernatural existence. He takes us to a location that holds the secret to the supernatural. The writer reveals to us the meaning and message we can find when we find ourselves on what has been called the true and spiritual Mount Zion. We read in Hebrews 12:18–22,

> For you have not come to a mountain that can be touched and to a blazing fire, and to darkness and gloom and whirlwind, and to the blast of a trumpet and the sound of words which sound was such that those who heard begged that no further word be spoken to them. For they could not bear the command, "If even a beast touches the mountain, it will be stoned." And so terrible was the sight, that Moses said, "I am full of fear and trembling." But you have come to Mount Zion and to the city of the living God, the heavenly Jerusalem, and to myriads of angels . . .

As you can easily see from this passage, many of the Hebrew saints were operating from the wrong vantage point—very similar to how many of us are today. They were functioning from the wrong realm. This wrong realm was known as Mount Sinai.

For historical context, Mount Sinai was the mountain where Moses was given the Ten Commandments. Mount Sinai symbolized the location where Israel had been informed on how to operate as a nation. Thunder had roared, the ground had shook, and fire had blazed as God had come to that mountain. In fact, people ran away in both terror and fear. They had run due to their feelings of insecurity and uncertainty. They had run because the very awesomeness of God had disturbed them. As a result, they were unable to find rest in that place.

To bring the imagery and meaning of Mount Sinai forward into our contemporary context, it would be similar to Christians living today from an earthly perspective. It means using the physical world—the world of the five senses—to govern thoughts and decisions. To stand on Mount Sinai means to stand with your feet firmly planted on the ground. It means that decisions are made, actions are taken, and perspective is derived from an earth-bound orientation.

The believers being addressed in the book of Hebrews, like many believers today, were so earth-bound by their circumstances that they were operating from the perspective of the wrong mountain. The author of Hebrews set out to change the perspective of their location. He reminded them that they had come to a new mountain—a new realm known as the mountain of Zion.

One of the worst things in the world is to be lost. One of the most unsettling feelings is when you don't know where you are and don't know how to get where you need to go. It brings up so much uncertainty within. To be located in one place but have the need to be operating from another place yet not knowing how to get there can carry with it an atmosphere of chaos. The believers at the time of Hebrews were lost on Mount Sinai. They were far removed from where they needed to be functioning, which was on Mount Zion. In order for them to find their way and maximize their experience in this life, they needed to relocate. They needed to not only find the path but also take it to the other mountain. They needed to realize their position on Mount Zion.

All of this raises the question: What's so special about Mount Zion? You may recall the song often sung in churches about marching to Mount Zion as well as the references to it as the "beautiful city of God." But did you know that as a believer in Jesus Christ, you don't need to march there at all? In fact, as a believer in Jesus Christ, you are already on Mount Zion. You are already standing in that realm. You don't have to travel to it. You don't have to find your way there. You don't have to strap on your hiking boots. You are on Mount Zion.

For starters, Mount Zion is the heavenly kingdom realm of God's holy presence. It represents a spiritual perspective. It represents a spiritual orientation. It is not the realm of rules, laws, and regulations or the realm of sacrifices. Mount Zion reflects your position in Jesus Christ.

Mount Zion is a place where you feel led to worship. It is where we read that David brought the Ark of the Covenant in 2 Samuel 6:16–17:

> Then it happened as the ark of the Lord came into the city of David that Michal the daughter of Saul looked out of the window and saw King David leaping and dancing before the Lord; and she despised him in her heart. So they brought in the ark of the Lord and set it in its place inside the tent which David had pitched for it; and David offered burnt offerings and peace offerings before the Lord.

David didn't contain his worship before the Lord. He leaped and he danced in celebration. The first thing I want to underscore about Mount Zion is that it should evoke a response in you. After all, it is the realm of God's presence. Anytime you are in God's presence, it ought to inspire you to worship. You can't be on Mount Zion and not worship because God's presence creates a spirit of worship within each of us. Thus, one very easy way to determine if you are living your life from this spiritual realm is by asking whether or not you regularly worship. If there is little or no worship in your life, you are not functioning from the realm of Mount Zion. Zion is the place where God dwells.

Scripture speaks to the importance of worship throughout its pages. The Bible tells us that God seeks worshippers (John 4:23). He desires hearts that desire Him. And even though God has all the worship from the angels that He could ever need, He still desires that we worship Him as His followers. He desires our worship because we are the only ones created with a choice. Humanity has been gifted with free will. Our worship brings God joy because it comes from a decision within each of us to recognize who He is, what He has done, and what we are trusting Him to do.

When you worship, you honor God. But did you know that when you worship, you also honor yourself? The reason I can say you also honor yourself is because it is in worshipping God that you set yourself up to reclaim what the enemy has stolen. When you worship, you release kingdom authority into your life to defeat the opposition through the power tied to authentic worship.

Some people think that worship is just about singing. They think it's about attending church. They think listening to a sermon checks off the box of "going to worship." But worship is about much more than all of that. Worship involves your heart. It involves your emotions. David set a great example of worship when he danced before the Lord. Worship is not something that is done for you. Worship always needs to be done by you and is part of your lifestyle if it is to be considered true worship.

Yet in addition to being a place of worship, Mount Zion also represents a place of God's rule and governance (Isa. 24:23; Ps. 74:2). It indicates a location for rule and authority. We see this in Psalm 110:1–2, where it says, "The LORD says to my Lord: 'Sit at My right hand until I make Your enemies a footstool for Your feet.' The LORD will stretch forth Your strong scepter from Zion, saying, 'Rule in the midst of your enemies.'"

Read that last line again: Rule in the midst of your enemies. Doesn't that give you confidence? Doesn't that create a stirring within you to enable you to believe that you can overcome that which comes against you? I don't know what may be coming against you, but Mount Zion is the place to overrule it. Mount Zion is the place where God says you can rule in the midst of your enemies. But you won't tap into that rule to release it if you don't first worship. Because if God can't get you to worship Him, why would He trust you to rule on His behalf? If your worship is all about you— your name, your notoriety, your pleasure, your profile—then won't your rule be carried out to simply promote yourself all the more?

What you worship reveals what you want. And God only gives the authority of His rule to those who want Him first (Matt. 6:33).

Mount Zion is the place God has ordained to be used to overrule that which seeks to overrule each one of us. Whether it comes in through your own emotions, family, your finances, mind, or your circumstances, Satan seeks to trip each of us up. But God has established Mount Zion as His realm of governance where believers can tap into His presence and overrule Satan's strategies through the divine governance of kingdom authority. The scepter of God's rule is in Zion. Psalm 132:13–14 puts it like this: "For the Lord has chosen Zion; He has desired it for His habitation. This is My resting place forever; here I will dwell, for I have desired it." Ultimately, He hangs out where He is getting worship from worshippers.

So far we've seen that Mount Zion starts off as a place where God is worshipped. Next, we have learned that it is also a place where God overrules all, even in the midst of your enemies. But according to Psalm 132:13–14, we discover that it is also a place where you can find rest. And when I say rest, I'm not talking about sleep. I'm talking about the rest we read about in Hebrews 4:9–11: "So there remains a Sabbath rest for the people of God. For the one who has entered His

> What you worship reveals what you want. And God only gives the authority of His rule to those who want Him first (Matt. 6:33).

rest has himself also rested from his works, as God did from His. Therefore, let us be diligent to enter that rest, so that no one will fall, through following the same example of disobedience."

Rest occurs when God takes over a situation on your behalf. Rest happens when you don't have to force things to happen. It shows up when you know that God is handling everything on your behalf. Rest is similar to what God told the Israelites they would find when they arrived in the Promised Land. He told them they would arrive to a place where there would be wells they did not have to dig, or land they did not have to farm. They would find cattle they did not have to raise and houses they did not have to build. The Promised Land was a land of rest. It was a land of provision.

Do you know God has already set up some things for you as well just like He did for the Israelites? It may not be a well, farm, or cattle, but it will give you rest. He has already prepared your path before you have even taken one step on it at all. But if He can't get you to worship Him or surrender to His will and His rule, then you will never wake up to realize you are at your Promised Land on Zion. You will never get to experience all that has been chosen for you to have and experience.

If you don't know you are already there in Christ Jesus, you will never learn to operate from there. If you fail to operate from there, then you will never get the benefits of there even though you are there. Your mind, heart, and senses will be clouded with the circumstances of the world in which you live that you will fail to recognize the unseen, spiritual world behind it all.

One time when I visited the Golden Gate Bridge in San Francisco, the cloud cover was so thick that you could not even see the bridge at all. This massive structure, which can be seen for miles, or even from a plane, could not be seen at all by all of us standing just hundreds of yards away from it. These clouds didn't care that thousands of people had traveled there at that time just to see the bridge. The clouds were doing what clouds do. Because of their presence, people did not get to experience the bridge like they had hoped.

Similarly, when you or I fail to recognize our true position in the heavenly realm with Christ—and as a result, we neglect to view life and make decisions out of this authoritative position—then the worries of this world become condensation on our soul's eyes. The distractions, demands, and difficulties we face create clouds that cover and conceal the spiritual world and our relationship with it. It doesn't matter if you made every intention to get up and go to church, or go to Bible study, or set out on a spiritual quest—if the clouds are covering the spiritual realm so much so that you can no longer even recognize it, you will miss what you had set out to see. In fact, all God has for you—all the good plans He has for you—can be right there in front of you, so close that you can nearly touch them, but if they're hidden by the clouds of human wisdom rather than revealed by the clarity of another realm, you'll miss them entirely.

In order to see clearly as you navigate through this life, you must look with heavenly eyes. You must realize you have already been repositioned when you were raised together in Christ in the spiritual realm. But if you do not operate spiritually—from this spiritual realm—you will fail to tap into the authority tied to this location. You will fail to even know where it is or how to access it. What's worse, you will fail to actualize God's great power in your everyday experiences.

There is nothing quite like witnessing God work something out for you that you could not work out for yourself. There is nothing like experiencing God's unseen reality influencing your seen existence. But that cannot take place unless you first recognize how to see all of life from the spiritual realm. Until you learn to function from the realm of Zion.

This concept of kingdom authority involves God's process of bringing heaven's rule into history. It is God bringing the principles and benefits of eternity into time. That's what kingdom authority is all about. But the only way to use God's authority on your own behalf is to move out of one system—the clouded world's system that leaves God out. You must move out of the cloud and into the clear skies of the spiritual system of God's unseen realm. Isaiah 2:1–4 explains this for us:

The word which Isaiah the son of Amoz saw concerning Judah and Jerusalem.

"Now it will come about that
In the last days
The mountain of the house of the LORD
Will be established as the chief of the mountains,
And will be raised above the hills;

And all the nations will stream to it.
And many peoples will come and say,
'Come, let us go up to the mountain of the LORD,
To the house of the God of Jacob;
That He may teach us concerning His ways
And that we may walk in His paths.'
For the law will go forth from Zion
And the word of the LORD from Jerusalem.
And He will judge between the nations,
And will render decisions for many peoples;
And they will hammer their swords into plow-
    shares and their spears into pruning hooks.
Nation will not lift up sword against nation,
And never again will they learn war."

There is a lot in this passage to take in, but I want you to start off by noticing that in Zion, there is a mountain. In the Bible, mountains often refer to kingdoms. And kingdoms refer to realms of authority. They exist as systems of authority from which a ruler reigns. In the world today, we know all too well what happens when systems of authority change. We know what happens when rule is transferred from one system to another. All you have to do is look at an election. Anytime there is a rule change due to an election, the entire staffing and administration changes with it. There is a shift in authority that affects everyone and everything.

When you and I recognize that we have come to Mount Zion, by virtue of our relationship with Jesus Christ, we have instituted a rule change. We have invited an authority change. We have opened the door to understanding that operating from the spiritual perspective of Zion means operating under God's administration and not the world's. All must change, not just your stated allegiance. Because in order to experience God's kingdom authority in your life, you must also abide in and align under His authoritative administration and His rules.

Living in light of Zion means that when God's law, rules, governance, and guidelines come into play, you align your life choices consistently with them. Zion becomes the Chief Mountain of your life. Zion becomes the preeminent kingdom of your experiences. God Himself becomes the overriding authority in all you think, say, and do. And unless and until that is your perspective, you will never experience God's kingdom power over all that needs to be overruled in the world of your five senses.

If all you are is a heavenly saint on Sunday but then revert back to living hell-bent and earth-bound on Monday, you'll only tap into what earth has to offer you because you only get the power of Zion from the position of Zion. You only get the gift of God's rule when you make contact with His glory through your worship in His presence. God wants to join you at work, in your home, in your relationships. He wants to hang out with you so that you can experience the power of His presence. But He will only hang out with you if you will hang out with Him. That shouldn't be too hard to understand.

Everyone reading this book can probably remember a younger sibling or cousin who wanted to hang out with the older kids but the older kids didn't want to hang out with them. Or, maybe you were the younger sibling or cousin. But even though the younger child wanted to hang out with the others, since the older teens didn't want the younger kid around, it just turned into a "tag-along" situation rather than truly hanging out together. God is too great to lower Himself to the level of a tag-along in your life. He will hang out with you and reveal His power and kingdom authority to you but only to the degree that you desire Him to by seeking to hang out with Him on Zion and come into agreement with what is happening in heaven.

As we saw earlier in Hebrews 12, God has a lot to give you when you meet Him in the spiritual realm of Zion. One of the things He gives is His rest in this place of His presence. He takes you deeper with Him when you are in His heavenly city—the New Jerusalem—known as Zion. But even beyond the rest He can supply, we learn in Hebrews 12:22 that it is in this spiritual realm that we also come into the presence of a myriad of angels. Not only do you get God's presence, but you also get the presence of His angels.

As Hebrews 1:14 tells us, every believer has been assigned an angel. Every believer has an angel whose job it is to assist in working out God's will and plan in their lives. You can consider your angel like a delivery person of sorts. This angel has been specifically assigned to bring you the messages and assistance for the furthering of God's manifest will in your life. But this angel is limited to your location and alignment under God. If you are not at home in the presence of God on Zion, just like a person delivering certified mail to you cannot get you what you need if you are not at your physical home, you will miss the delivery. When you and I choose to operate out of sync with the governance of God, we limit our own involvement with the support of His angels.

Your ability to experience God's authority on earth is tied to the degree to which you are connected to what the angels are doing in heaven. If you are not connected to what they are doing up there, then you will not experience their work on God's behalf down here. There must exist that link with heaven for you to access God's plan unfolding for you. The reason this link exists is because of God's goal to connect heaven and earth. He is seeking to connect what happens up there with what happens down here. What happens in heaven shouldn't stay in heaven. Rather, God tells us that He desires that His kingdom will come and His will should be done on earth as it is in heaven (Matt. 6:10). God wants heaven and earth to exist on the same page. The reason He wants earth on the same page as heaven is because heaven is perfect.

No one leans to their own understanding in heaven. No one argues with God's will or God's way in heaven. The reason heaven is perfect is because God's rule is followed perfectly. For earth to reflect heaven more so, and for your life to tap into the kingdom authority that flows from God's throne, you need to let your secular thinking go. You need to let your worldly wisdom disappear. You need to release your educational conflicts with God. You need to surrender the perspectives you got from your parents and align yourself with God's Word. If you want to fully flesh out the effects of kingdom authority in your life, you need to let all the stuff that belongs to earth go. Just let it go. Only when you operate from a mindset of the spiritual realm, rooted and grounded in Christ and His Word, will you experience all God has available for you.

We also see from Hebrews 12 that God renders judgment for believers from Mount Zion. This divine intervention is supported by saints who have already gone to glory. These are the general assembly and church of the firstborn enrolled in heaven (v. 23). This cloud of witnesses joins Jesus in interceding for believers on earth for the execution of kingdom authority in their lives (v. 1).

Of utmost importance is the ongoing work of the blood of Jesus that releases testimony so God can act with authority on behalf of believers giving the Father the legal right to forgive sin. Jesus's mediatorial work (Matt. 28:19–20; 1 Tim. 2:5) connects us to our sacred covenantal bond with God for the exercise of kingdom authority from heaven into history (Heb. 12:24).

One of my great joys over the years was serving as the chaplain for the Dallas Cowboys. I served in that role for numbers of years, and as an avid fan of football, it was always something I loved to do. As the chaplain, when I was much younger, I would actually attend their official practices from time to time and work out with the guys. Sometimes I would even run to catch a pass from Roger Staubach! I would be running alongside Drew Peterson or Tony Hill. Those were great times.

But one of the plays that has always stuck with me that I learned during those days is called the fly pattern. A fly pattern is where you try to throw a touchdown in one play. The way you do this is when the quarterback gets the ball, he runs back a bit. While he's dropping back, the receiver is running down the field to get ready. The quarterback then throws the ball when the receiver is ready with the goal of getting it just right so that the receiver can score.

The problem in executing a fly pattern, though, is that the linebackers on the defense don't want it executed. So these linebackers will do everything in their power, within the rules of the game, to disturb the play. They will rush the passer. They may blitz. They can jump to deflect the ball. But when the quarterback sees that the defense is on their game and he doesn't stand a chance to get the ball downfield, he turns to what is called a waggle. What's interesting about the waggle is that it is still designed to score a touchdown. The waggle is meant to replace the fly pattern when the fly pattern won't work out.

The reason I love these two plays is because it reminds me of how God called a touchdown pass on Mount Sinai. He told Israel that He was going to throw them the ball. He wanted them to catch the kingdom and all it means, while bringing in the rule of God. The problem is that Satan blitzed the play. Satan got in the backfield, and he canceled the first play out. In fact, Satan probably thought the play was over altogether when he tacked Jesus on the cross. But what he didn't realize is that God had a waggle. God knew there was another way to get the touchdown. This waggle is what we have just been reading about on Mount Zion. It is available to us through our faith in Jesus Christ and the forgiveness He has given us for our sins. The victory we all desire is found in this one place. Zion is the place of kingdom authority in Jesus's name. That's why each of us needs to prioritize the worship of God's person, the alignment under God's rule, and the perspective of heaven in our lives, based on His Word. When you do that, you will begin to see that which is more spectacular than you could ever have imagined. You will see God authorizing His kingdom power from heaven for use on earth.

CHAPTER SIX

The Ruler

 On July 11, 1963, George Wallace stood in front of the University of Alabama to deny black students the opportunity to attend college there. His famous statement, which has echoed harshly throughout the hallways of time, was, "Segregation yesterday, today, and forever!" Wallace sought to use his authority as the governor of Alabama to continue an illegitimate division based on historical inequity. Wallace even had his support team there to affirm his decision of denial.

Everything went according to Wallace's plan, until Washington, DC, stepped in. When the higher authority of President John F. Kennedy showed up, represented through one hundred troops who came to town to overrule what Wallace had declared, all bets were off. Wallace had made a claim that would affect thousands of lives by maintaining a standard of injustice in that state. But to over-turn that claim, there had to be a higher level of authority than his own—that of being the governor of Alabama. This higher author-ity had to possess the power to undo the illegitimate claims and rule of George Wallace. And, thankfully, it did.

Similarly, we all have an enemy who has tried to use his power and deception to push us down and keep us out of places where we rightfully belong. The evil one has stood at the door of our lives with one overriding goal. Satan wants to block God's kingdom purposes for each one of us. He wants to block our divine reasons for being, both individually and also collectively. Satan wants nothing more than to bully you into steering away from God's pre-ordained design for your life. Satan takes great delight in keeping you from experienc-ing all that God has established for you. Or, if you do eventually get to experience it, he will be satisfied with riddling it with so much trial, turmoil, and difficulty that you miss out on the joy tied to it.

> The evil one has stood at the door of our lives with one overriding goal. Satan wants to block God's kingdom purposes for each one of us.

Like George Wallace's formidable frame postured at the door of the university decades ago, Satan stands strong at the door of your existence, unwilling to budge. Like a bully, he wants to make sure what has been written about you and your divine destiny in your book in the heavenly realm is not actualized. Satan won't back down, at least not based on what you or I do or say on our own. He will only move when we learn how to access a Higher Authority than him.

Until we learn to do that, Satan is free to stir up all manner of destruction in your life. As part of his design to get you off course, he wants you to have sicknesses that are outside of God's preferred will. So, he will lead you down paths of physical destruction and stress to wear down your body and make it more prone to illness or disease, or he wants you to have discouragement, pain, and relational breakdown that will negatively impact your mental well-being. Satan seeks an early death or demise for all believers. He regularly seeks to draw us into sin to disrupt our fellowship with God. And if he can't get that, he will settle for the death or demise of hopes, health, and harmony instead. He'll do anything to get and keep a follower of Jesus off track. Satan is trying to keep you off track and prevent you from walking through the doors to experience your full kingdom purpose in life.

Now, before I go much further, I want to clarify something. I am not saying that every sickness, disappointment, difficulty, or death is outside of God's preferred will. God often sovereignly allows these challenges and losses in our lives for His purposes, as He works them out for good, causing us to be conformed to the image of Christ (Rom. 8:28–29). But it is true that some sicknesses, disappointments, difficulties, and even death *do* take place outside of God's preferred will. The reason is a result of being successfully interfered with by Satan or his demons. Satan has a well-rehearsed and uncanny ability to block God's purposes and stifle a believer's right relationship with God when we yield to his deception.

While that is a discouraging and troubling truth to realize, there is also good news: you have access to the kingdom authority you need to silence the accuser and get him to step aside. To whatever degree that Satan is bringing havoc into your life, God has come up with a legislative mechanism endowed to you to keep Satan from robbing you of God's will, purposes, and plan. This legislative mechanism is what we know as spiritual authority.

The book of Revelation provides us with some of the greatest insights into the battles that take place for spiritual authority. It goes into many of the dirty details involved in the clash of kingdoms taking place all around us. The book of Revelation is a statement book, not only about this war in the heavenly realm, but about God's ultimate kingdom authority. We can see throughout its pages that Satan will be removed after the time of tribulation. He will be defeated once and for all. But what we also see is that unfortunately right now Satan is free to roam. In fact, he even has access to enter into heaven and stir up trouble if he likes. A perfect example of this is found in Job 1:6–7:

> Now there was a day when the sons of God came to present themselves before the LORD, and Satan also came among them. The LORD said to Satan, "From where do you come?" Then Satan answered the LORD and said, "From roaming about on the earth and walking around on it."

Satan came from his location of roaming around the earth and presented himself before the Lord. Access to God is clearly his to use whenever he wants to accuse someone of something or ask permission from God to trip someone up, like he did with Simon Peter (Luke 22:31–32). Yet while Satan can come and go as he pleases in carrying out his schemes, we discover in the book of Revelation some strategies on how to defeat him. We discover these strategies especially in Revelation chapter 12.

This unique, and often overlooked, chapter gives us a glimpse into the cosmic clash that our eyes cannot see and our ears do not hear, even though it is a clash raging all around us. Reading Revelation gives us a peek into that which is beyond our natural ability to recognize or see physically. It also helps us to more fully understand our role in this unseen drama playing out so we will be able to wield the power and authority given to us in the name of Jesus. This is important to know because if and when we try to fight Satan in our own strength, or in any other way than what God has prescribed, Satan will win. You and I are no match for the devil. But we can take comfort in knowing that God has given us access to His power and kingdom authority, which is able to take Satan down. Let's look at this more closely in Revelation 12:7–12:

> And there was war in heaven, Michael and his angels waging war with the dragon. The dragon and his angels waged war, and they were not strong enough, and there was no longer a place found for them in heaven. And the great dragon was thrown down, the serpent of old who is called the devil

and Satan, who deceives the whole world; he was thrown down to the earth, and his angels were thrown down with him. Then I heard a loud voice in heaven, saying,

"Now the salvation, and the power, and the kingdom of our God and the authority of His Christ have come, for the accuser of our brethren has been thrown down, he who accuses them before our God day and night. And they overcame him because of the blood of the Lamb and because of the word of their testimony, and they did not love their life even when faced with death. For this reason, rejoice, O heavens and you who dwell in them. Woe to the earth and the sea, because the devil has come down to you, having great wrath, knowing that he has only a short time".

This is the spiritual battle going on all around us. In the description of it, we can clearly see Satan's strategies. His job is to prevent God's followers from experiencing what He has done for them, and he seeks to do this through deception. He is an accuser and a deceiver. In fact, it's Satan's goal to deceive the whole world. That means none of us are exempt. If you are here, then you are in the world. If you are in the world, then that means you are subject to Satan's schemes of deception. And his schemes are legion.

You and I are living in a day of mass deception. People are being tricked about their gender and identity. They are being deceived about the definition of a family or marriage. People are being hoodwinked on how to handle their finances. The world's population is facing an onslaught of deception all the while buying it hook, line, and sinker. We are being duped by the devil, all the while claiming to know "my truth." In fact, people will defend their truth to the death these days. Unfortunately, it is often to their own death—whether a death of emotional well-being, health, financial stability, relational harmony, cultural chaos, or even physical death.

Satan has gotten very good at his game. When he can manipulate and twist our thoughts—whether that relates to us individually, or in families, at work or even in church—he advances his evil agenda. Satan feeds off of the devastation and destruction he creates. We read in 1 Peter 5:8, "Be of sober spirit, be on the alert. Your adversary, the devil, prowls around like a roaring lion, seeking someone to devour." Keep in mind, an *adversary* and *accuser* are both legal terms. They have to do with the complainant in a lawsuit.

Satan doesn't want to just bully us to get us to cry. Rather, he seeks to defeat each of us legally. He wants a legal claim to his victories over God's followers. It's only when he gets a legal claim, due to our actual or potential sins (2 Cor. 12:7), and we are unaware of how to counter that claim through accessing kingdom authority, that he prevents us from living out our divine design. For Christians, he wants to keep us from fulfilling God's plan for our lives during our time on earth. For non-Christians, he wants to keep them from becoming Christians.

But we do hear hope in the passage in Revelation describing the cosmic clash of kingdoms: "And they overcame him . . ." (12:11). To overcome means to prevail against one's opposition or circumstances. It includes prevailing against, over, or through. You and I, as followers of Jesus Christ, have the ability to prevail. But one quick look around the culture, or one quick scroll on any social media feed, will reveal that Satan is prevailing on a lot of levels. He is winning. He is beating out many believers in that which is illegitimate and against the will of God. He is blocking the spiritual progress of myriads of people worldwide.

And since this is so easy to spot and identify, it may cause you to wonder why. Why is Satan winning in so many ways? Or, why is God taking so long to kick him to the curb? Why is so much allowed to take place that is obviously outside of the preferred will of God? The reason why is also found in his power to deceive, which we read just a little bit ago. This passage lists three specific things believers are to do to overcome the attacks of the evil one, and I'd like to go through each one right now.

It's critical to know these three things because Satan isn't defeated just because you want him to be defeated. Neither is he defeated just because you have an awareness of God's greater power. Like in any battle, sporting event, or war, here are strategies and methodologies that take place in order to secure a victory. Spiritual war is no different. Let's spend the remainder of our time together in this chapter looking at the three steps to silencing Satan and overcoming his deceptive schemes.

The first thing you need to know is that it's all about the blood. I'm sure you've either heard or sung the hymn, "There's power, power, wonder-working power in the precious blood of the Lamb."

The blood refers to the sacrificial cross of Christ. His sacrificial death on the cross that brought about the shedding of His blood is more than a religious symbol. It's power. Jesus's blood is spiritual authority.

That's why we read in Hebrews 12:24 that Christ's blood is tied to the new covenant. It says, ". . . and to Jesus, the mediator of a new covenant, and to the sprinkled blood, which speaks better than *the blood* of Abel." It's important to know that blood talks. Christ's blood talks. And it speaks better than the blood of Abel, or anyone or anything else. To understand why Christ's blood is compared to Abel's in this passage, we need to turn a few pages back in the Bible to Hebrews 11:4. This is where we read, "By faith Abel offered to God a better sacrifice than Cain, through which he obtained the testimony that he was righteous, God testifying about his gifts, and through faith, though he is dead, he still speaks."

If you are unfamiliar with the story, let me catch you up. Cain and Abel were the sons of Adam and Eve. Cain killed Abel when he became jealous of God's acceptance of Abel's worship. So, when we read in the book of Hebrews that though Abel is dead, he still speaks, it is referring to the message of Abel. We find this message in Genesis 4:9–10, which says, "Then the LORD said to Cain, 'Where is Abel your brother?' And he said, 'I do not know. Am I my brother's keeper?' He said, 'What have you done? The voice of your brother's blood is crying to Me from the ground.'" It is Abel's blood that spoke on his behalf to tell of the murderous sins of Cain.

In fact, it was Abel's blood that convicted Cain for what he had done and ushered in his sentence. We read about this in Genesis 4:11–12: "Now you are cursed from the ground, which has opened its mouth to receive your brother's blood from your hand. When you cultivate the ground, it will no longer yield its strength to you; you will be a vagrant and a wanderer on the earth." Abel's blood condemned Cain to a lifetime of pain and suffering. Abel's blood spoke judgment on his brother Cain.

Thus, if Jesus's blood speaks better than Abel's blood, what is His blood saying? What Jesus's blood is saying is that it overrules the condemnation due us for our sins. As we read in Romans 8:1, "Therefore there is now no condemnation for those who are in Christ Jesus." Abel's blood showed up in the courtroom of heaven to give testimony to Cain's guilt. Jesus's blood testifies in the same courtroom so that we may have forgiveness and pardon when we have trusted in Him for the salvation of our souls. Jesus's blood overrules the accuser. Jesus's blood silences the prosecution. Jesus's blood protects, delivers, and empowers those who have placed faith in Him. His blood is the power of His sacrifice, which operates today on behalf of anyone who needs it and places their faith in Him to receive it. Jesus's blood pronounces judgment on Satan in the courtroom of heaven.

Another example of the power of the blood shows up in Exodus 12, which looks at the Passover. It is when God planned to take the life of every firstborn Egyptian in His plan to set His people free. So as to protect the firstborn of the Jews, God asked them to slay a pure animal sacrifice and place the blood over the doorposts of the home. When the death angel came to their home, the death angel would see the blood and pass over them. In other words, the death angel needed to see the identification of the sacrifice in order to withhold the judgment of death. Similarly, you and I are covered by the blood of Jesus when we have trusted in Him for our salvation. When Satan seeks to destroy us or bring about deadly plans against us by accusing us spiritually in the courtroom of heaven to get us off track from God's preferred will for our lives, Jesus's blood can stop Satan in his tracks. Yet if he doesn't see Jesus's blood covering us through rightly aligning underneath His rule, he will be free to carry out his schemes. The cross of Christ grants the believer the right to activate the legal transaction of Calvary through confession and repentance (1 John 1:9).

It is the blood that defeats Satan because of what the blood means. Colossians 1:13 tells us what Jesus did for us when we read, "For He rescued us from the domain of darkness, and transferred us to the kingdom of His beloved Son . . ." Jesus's blood rescued us from the dominion of Satan and relocated us under the rule of the kingdom of God Himself.

We read more about this in Colossians 2:13–15:

When you were dead in your transgressions and the uncircumcision of your flesh, He made you alive together with Him, having forgiven us all our transgressions, having canceled out the certificate of debt consisting of decrees against us, which was hostile to us; and He has taken it out of the way, having nailed it to the cross. When He had disarmed the rulers and authorities, He made a public display of them, having triumphed over them through Him.

No matter what Satan can write up about you—all of the accusations he can summon, whether a lie or truth—Jesus's sacrificial work on the cross has "canceled" it out. The legal accusations against you no longer stand spiritually when you come under the blood of the Lamb. Jesus did this by disarming Satan and his minions, stripping them of any rightful authority to condemn anyone who places faith in Christ alone for the forgiveness of sins. That's why Satan spends so much of his time trying to deceive us. It's what he has left in his arsenal. Satan doesn't have any rightful spiritual authority over anyone who is in Jesus Christ. So he seeks to trick us instead. The problem is that he's very good at deception, and far too many of us fall for it hook, line, and sinker.

For example, if someone were to pull a gun on you and tell you to sit down, you might just do it. If you had nothing with which to defend yourself, you might go ahead and sit down. In fact, you'll probably do a lot of what they tell you to do because there is a gun pointing at you. But let's say you were to discover there were no bullets in the gun—what would happen then? Or what if you discovered the gun wasn't even real? I imagine that would change the entire equation. If the person holding the gun said to sit, you might not sit. Or if they said to jump, you might not jump. The reason why you would no longer regularly cooperate is because you would know you had been tricked.

On the cross, Christ took the bullets out of Satan's gun. He stripped him of the weapons he would use to control and condemn you. Yet while Jesus disarmed Satan, removing him of his authority, He didn't remove his power to deceive. Satan still has deceiving power, and he uses it all of the time. He just can't rule you if you know your legal recourse for defeating him. That's why the blood is so important. That's why Revelation 12 says, "And they overcame him because of the blood of the Lamb . . ." (v. 11).

But just because Satan has been disarmed doesn't mean he acts like it. Satan doesn't want you or anyone to know he's been disarmed. So he wields his empty gun around trying to get you, and other Christians, to cower. It is the blood of Jesus that gives you the authority you need to access a higher authority than Satan. Not only that, but Revelation 12:11 goes on to tell us the second thing we can use to overcome Satan's schemes and legal accusations, and that is "the word of their testimony."

Again, a legal term is used in this passage to reinforce the truth that Satan is a legally defeated adversary. A testimony is what is used in court to either convict someone or prove innocence of someone. So while Satan is busy accusing you in the high courtroom of heaven, just know you have both the legal recourse of Jesus's blood that speaks on your behalf as well as the word of your testimony. You can testify against Satan. You do this by going to the written and living Word of God and testifying to the truth of God. It is the Word of God that carries the legal weight in the spiritual realm. In fact, the only testimony received in God's courtroom is the testimony that is consistent with the laws of the Court.

When Jesus was tempted by the devil, Jesus didn't sit down to reason with Satan. He didn't tell him what popular opinion or the talking heads were spewing at the moment. No, Jesus went to the written Word. The Living Word referenced the written Word to shut Satan down. Three times Jesus quoted Scripture in response to Satan's attempt to lure Him into sin. Three times in Matthew 4 Jesus said:

- "It is written . . ." (v. 4)
- "It is written . . ." (v. 7)
- "It is written . . ." (v. 10)

And the devil left Him. Satan got lost because Satan is allergic to the Scripture. He can't handle spiritual truth. So whenever you need to overcome Satan's strategies against you, just know that you can always rely on the Word of God. You can give a testimony to what God says, and that will grant you kingdom authority in the courtroom on high. You'll never have kingdom authority when you rely on human testimony or a human perspective. In fact, the Bible calls human wisdom what it is: demonic. James 3:15 puts it like this: "This wisdom is not that which comes down from above, but is earthly, natural, demonic." James tells us that kind of thinking is rooted in hell. Whenever you give a perspective that disagrees with God's, it's rooted in hell. What's more, it carries no weight in heaven's courtroom as Satan stands to accuse you.

The "word of your testimony" also means there must be a willingness to publicly identify with the living word of God, Jesus Christ. If you want to activate the power of the blood, your words need to be about Jesus. God, the Father, didn't die on the cross. The Holy Spirit didn't shed His blood on the cross. It is Jesus who shed His blood. It is Jesus's name you need to publicly declare to access the kingdom authority needed to silence Satan in the heavenly courts. It is Jesus who said, "All authority has been given to Me in heaven and on earth" (Matt. 28:18b). If you want to exercise victory over the devil, you need to publicly proclaim the name of Jesus. Jesus made it clear our public identification with Him determines whether He uses His kingdom authority to act on our behalf (Matt. 10:22–23).

The third thing we discover in Revelation 12:11 that will enable us to overcome Satan in the spiritual courts is a relinquishing of love for our own lives. We read, ". . . and they did not love their life even when faced with death." I realize that may sound like a lot to ask, especially in today's narcissist-bent social media culture. But it's in the Scripture, and it is a key truth to accessing the kingdom authority necessary for defeating Satan's attacks on your life. To

> It is Jesus's name you need to publicly declare to access the kingdom authority needed to silence Satan in the heavenly courts. It is Jesus who said, "All authority has been given to Me in heaven and on earth" (Matt. 28:18b).

illustrate this principle more clearly, I want to look at Jesus in the garden of Gethsemane. When He was about to be taken away and be crucified, He responded with surrender to God's will. Jesus didn't pretend to be thrilled about the concept of the cross. He remained authentic to His emotions and what He was facing. But He also surrendered them beneath God's will.

We read in Luke 22:42, "Father, if You are willing, remove this cup from Me; yet not My will, but Yours be done." Jesus laid down His love for His own life beneath His love for God's will and His kingdom agenda. The problem many, if not most, of us face in contemporary Christian culture is we have been lulled into believing it is the right thing to stand up for your will. It is the right thing to voice "your truth." It is the right thing to speak "your mind." We have gotten away from the concept of surrender. And that makes sense from a spiritual standpoint because of course Satan is going to encourage believers to choose their will over God's any and every day. But what we don't realize is that in doing so, Satan is stripping us of the keys we need for kingdom authority whenever we choose any other perspective than God's.

Surrender must take place for kingdom authority to show up in your life. Luke 9:23 explains surrender like this, through Jesus's own words: "And He was saying to them all, 'If anyone wishes to come after Me, he must deny himself, and take up his cross daily and follow Me.'" I want to encourage you to memorize this verse as well as to put it into practice. If you are going to get serious about your life as a Christian and seek to access the kingdom authority that is rightfully yours by virtue of Jesus, you need to make this verse real in your life. It can't merely be words on paper; it must be etched on your heart. Taking up your cross daily is an ongoing decision. It involves your public declaration and submission to the lordship of Jesus Christ.

When Jesus took up His cross, He walked down the road of suffering. He was accused of things He did not do, and yet He had to pay the price for the sins of the world on Calvary. To be a follower of Christ is to carry the connection with His declaration. That He is Lord over all. That He is the one true God. That He is the King of kings. It means being identified with Jesus, no matter the price tag for the identification.

This verse isn't calling you to physically die daily. It is calling you to identify with Jesus and His cross, no matter what it may cost you. You are not to love your own life—your pleasures, passions, or pursuits—more than you love Jesus Christ. Jesus has a lot of fans these days; He just doesn't have a lot of committed followers. There's a difference. A fan sits in the stands and watches the show or the game. A fan takes a backseat to analyze the activity on the field of play. But a follower gets down into the nitty gritty of the game. A follower puts in the work to represent Jesus in the best possible way. A follower publicly identifies with Jesus, whether it looks like he or she is winning or losing in life because of it.

What a lot of people want is a Jesus association without a Jesus identification. But God doesn't need more fans. He is looking for serious kingdom followers. Jesus doesn't desire convenient, casual, or cultural Christians. He wants biblical Christians willing to be linked up with Him. If you want to unleash the full experience of kingdom authority in your life, if you want to overcome Satan's accusations as he stands at the door of your purpose, significance,

> God doesn't need more fans. He is looking for serious kingdom followers. Jesus doesn't desire convenient, casual, or cultural Christians. He wants biblical Christians willing to be linked up with Him.

and destiny—you need to live covered under the blood of Jesus, while testifying to the work of Jesus and surrender your own life's desires under Christ's. When you do that, you will stop being a victim and walk tall as a victor. You will reclaim what the enemy has stolen, and then some. You will step into the hallways of a new opportunity as you witness the power from on high dispel and overturn the opposition in your pathway to a greater kingdom purpose. Being under Jesus's authority puts you over Satan's power so you can experience what it looks like when He vetoes the enemy's accusations against you.

CHAPTER SEVEN

The Restorer

 All of us have witnessed an implosion, either live or on television. We've seen what happens when people intentionally take down a building or a bridge. This is often done to clear the way for something new, or to remove a structure that has gotten old, worn down, and has become a risk and hazard. What once stood tall and strong is brought to the ground in a mere matter of seconds, by explosives. That which took months, or even years, to construct becomes dismantled instantaneously, turning into nothing more than the rubble of a collapse.

Implosions don't only take place in buildings, though. Implosions take place in lives. I'm sure you've seen this in the recent increase of scandalous stories coming to light, especially within Christendom. Pastors, leaders, seminary presidents, and even celebrities and secular business leaders have experienced a sudden implosion of all they had once worked so hard to achieve. These implosions have taken part due to sins committed in their pasts, which have come to the public light. Some have imploded based on things they have done while other people's lives have imploded based on things they have either said or posted online.

Yet outside of the public implosions of people around us, more personal and private implosions occur as well. In fact, many of us know what it is to have imploded dreams. You may know what it is like to have an imploded relationship, or an imploded hope and goal. All that you had worked so hard to achieve just collapses with one wrong move or decision. It's as if everything you had once invested has been wasted. Nothing stands to commemorate the blood, sweat, and tears you had once put in. It can bring both a headache and a heartache, or even a life-ache, when implosions take place.

It's at those moments in time when we long for a do-over. We wish we could turn back the hands of time so we could start all over again. But we soon discover time doesn't work that way. What's done has been done, and cannot be undone, no matter how hard we wish it to be so. And while some implosions take place because of our own decisions, there are still yet other implosions that come about from things that sit outside of our control. It could be a sudden death, accident, or situational downturn that rips the rug out from under your feet, leaving you to stand on the unsteadiness of uncertainty and loss.

Whether implosions are due to our own choices or outside circumstances, they hurt the same. You feel the angst. You wake up in the middle of the night because you hear the echoes of the explosions and the rumble of the crumbling concrete in your dreams. It's true that even years, or decades later, people can still feel the triggers of their trauma. We still grapple with the repercussions and the implications of the implosions that have taken place in our lives.

When a person stays in this state for too long, thoughts begin to consume them as they long for the rebuilding of what was torn down or lost. As you know, typically when a building or bridge is torn down, it is done so that something new can replace it. Yet far too often in our personal lives, we allow gaps to remain where things have imploded because we spend our time focusing on what we have lost rather than considering what we can now create in its place. It's only when we shift our thinking away from the implosion and more toward Christ and His kingdom that we discover that up from the ashes will arise something new.

Taking a look at Luke 22, we learn more about implosions and how we can approach them from a position of spiritual authority. We read about how someone who went down in shambles and had their life and purpose basically ripped from them can bounce back into someone even better than before. The context of the passage comes upon the heels of a debate. The disciples had been arguing, unsurprisingly, about who was going to be pegged the greatest in the kingdom of heaven. They've been vying for position by discussing the world's standards of significance. Yet while this debate occurs, Jesus enters the discussion and takes it into a whole new direction. He sees their pride. He hears their words of feigned superiority. He smells their conceit. So He intervenes.

"By the way, Simon," Jesus says—in my Tony Evans's translation. "Simon"—He says his name twice to be sure he's got his attention. Then He continues as the Bible records, ". . . behold, Satan has demanded permission to sift you like wheat" (Luke 22:31). Jesus set out to remind Simon (who would later go on to be called Simon Peter) that instead of arguing about who would be considered the greatest later on in glory, he might want to pay better attention to what's going on in the nasty here and now. He let him know the devil had come calling his name and had asked permission to go after him.

Satan wanted to sift Simon Peter like wheat.

The sifting process was the process of removing the chaff from the grain of wheat. It consisted of a tumultuous and often violent processing of shaking and disturbing things to remove the grain. This action separated the useful grain from the useless chaff. If we translate the goal of this process over to the human situation of Peter, we see that Satan's goal was to make Peter useless. He wanted to separate him from the purposes of the kingdom and discard him in the rubble of the chaff.

In fact, when chaff becomes separate from the grain, it will often simply blow away in the wind. Nothing can be done with it. It's empty of all value. But when we look more closely at the original language that the Scripture was written in, we see that Satan's goal didn't only involve Simon Peter. You can't tell that in English, but it's clearly visible in Greek. The word that was translated into *you* in verse 31 is actually a plural word in Greek. Jesus goes Texan on His disciples and throws out the word *y'all*. In the Greek, the verse would more literally read, "Simon, Simon, Satan has demanded permission to sift y'all like wheat."

If you recall at the start of this chapter, I mentioned that the disciples were gathered together debating who would be the greatest in the kingdom. Thus, when Jesus sought to redirect their thinking, He intentionally used a term that lumped them all together. The reason why Simon was called out first was the same reason he is usually called out first—Simon had proven by then to be a ringleader of the group. But after getting Simon's attention and settling down the discourse, Jesus made sure to mention that Satan's request to sift referred to all of them. The reason is that if Satan could sift them all, there would be no New Testament. There would be no Church age. There would be no continuation of the program of God because God built His program on the disciples. These are the men who would go on to be apostles and usher in the onset of Christianity as we know it today. In short, Satan's goal was to thwart the kingdom program of God.

It's no wonder why Satan wanted to sift them, shred them, and have their remains simply blow away in the wind. It's no wonder why Satan still wants to do that with all of us as kingdom followers today. Anytime he can make us useless for the advancement of God's kingdom, he is—by default—advancing his own. That's why

Satan seeks to thwart God's calling in your life and His vision for your dignity and destiny. He wants us all bound by traumas and triggers so deeply that we never amount to anything for the glory of God. Satan is after ruining every Christian's life who is reading this book. The plural "you" in Luke 22:31 refers to all of us. Satan has "demanded" to sift you, destroy you, and ruin you like chaff. Since he can't steal God's kingdom from Him, he's seeking to build his own. And he doesn't mind who he has to ruin to do it, or how long it might take.

After all, if you look at Simon Peter's life, you can see a pattern of attack. Satan made Simon a target from the start. We see his presence and persuasive powers at work in Peter's life as early as Matthew 16:21–23, where we read how Peter succumbs to Satan's deception but Jesus points it out:

> From that time Jesus began to show His disciples that He must go to Jerusalem, and suffer many things from the elders and chief priests and scribes, and be killed, and be raised up on the third day. Peter took Him aside and began to rebuke Him, saying, "God forbid it, Lord! This shall never happen to You." But He turned and said to Peter, "Get behind Me, Satan! You are a stumbling block to Me; for you are not setting your mind on God's interests, but man's."

Peter had the audacity to tell Jesus He was wrong. Think about that for a moment. Yet while it's easy to pin blame on Peter for something so absurd, how many times do we do the same thing? Any and every time we opt for our belief or perspective over Christ's, we are doing the same thing. We are telling Jesus that He is wrong. And Jesus's response to Peter will ring true for us as well. Jesus told Peter that the devil was controlling him. He wasn't about to listen to him or even argue with him when it was the devil speaking through him.

Similarly, whenever God says one thing and you say something else, the devil is controlling you. Whenever what you learn in school or online or on the news disagrees with what God's Word says and you buy into it, the devil is controlling you. Anytime your thoughts do not align with what God says, you have leaned into Satan's strategy of deception. Disagreeing with God is not independent thinking; it's demonic thinking. And every time you give in to demonic thinking, you open the door for Satan to legally demand to sift you more. Satan doesn't just show up out of nowhere when he comes for you. He looks for opportunities you and I have created for him because we've done something that has given him an "in." Our sin creates these open doors for Satan to do the shaking, tearing down, and ripping us apart from God's kingdom plan. This is why Scripture exhorts us not to give the devil an opportunity (Eph. 4:27).

So many people never actualize what God has for their lives because they are too caught up trying to pick up the rubble from the shifting and sifting Satan is doing. God gave Satan permission to sift Simon and the disciples. Just like He gave Satan permission to test Job and see what was in his heart. Satan may have demanded it, as in the case of the disciples, but it was still a request needing to be granted. God still had to give the okay to move forward with Satan's deceptive schemes and legal accusations. We must never forget that God is still sovereign over Satan.

Peter sought to keep the door opened to Satan's involvement when he continued thinking too highly of himself, even after Jesus's stern rebuke. We can see he didn't take Jesus seriously. Instead, he tried to defend himself. We read in Luke 22:33 that Peter didn't believe the sifting was for real. He retorted, "'Lord, with You I am ready to go both to prison and to death!'"

Rather than respond with humility, Peter chose pride. To which Jesus replied, "I say to you, Peter, the rooster will not crow today until you have denied three times that you know Me" (v. 34). Jesus saw through Peter's gusto and recognized it as a problem of independence, self-confidence, and brokenness. As talented and as self-confident as Peter was, how he felt about himself stood in his own way and needed to be addressed, and God would allow Satan to be His tool to address it. Peter thought he was all that, and a bag of chips! He viewed himself higher than he truly was and thus suffered from a pride complex. To put it lightly, he was braggadocious. Because of this, the door swung wide open for Satan to pursue tripping him up all the more. Satan had a case against Peter.

Have you ever promised God you would never do something only to wind up doing the very thing you said you would never do?

That's common to a lot of people. Pride comes before the fall. Pride acts as the dynamite used to cause the personal implosion. As Proverbs says, "Pride goes before destruction, and a haughty spirit before stumbling" (16:18). Peter told Jesus he would never deny Him. Jesus responded that he wouldn't even make it twenty-four hours before denying Him! I don't know about you, but if Jesus told me that I wouldn't make it twenty-four hours, I would probably have locked myself into a hotel room and not come out, but Peter didn't even bother to try to protect himself. He let his pride deceive him.

God will frequently grant Satan permission to sift those who need to be put in their place. God can use the devil to show you who you really are. He can allow the devil to break a brother or sister down so you can experience the growth that comes from surrender. Sure, Satan will provoke people or create situations through which to do his bidding, but he's the one behind it seeking to keep you defeated. While God is watching to see if you will rebuild something bigger and better than before. The choice is up to each one of us in how we respond after the implosions of our lives. We can sit, sulk, and sour. Or we can get up and grow up.

> God can use the devil to show you who you really are. He can allow the devil to break a brother or sister down so you can experience the growth that comes from surrender.

Far too often in spiritual warfare, we want to nurse our wounds rather than rebuild after a loss. We want to blame those through whom Satan moved. We think we are fighting people, systems, or even our own emotions. But in reality, God has allowed the devil to have his way with us in order to provide an opportunity for us to realign with God. Because of our innate connection with pride, God often accomplishes His purposes through our pain.

As we see in Peter's situation, he needed to be stripped of his self-sufficiency. That's what brokenness means. It means to learn the lesson that "apart from Me you can do nothing" (John 15:5). Brokenness means to understand that God is God and you aren't. This is an important lesson for each of us. It's a hard lesson, but it's critical for living out the fullness of your destiny. It's critical for accessing and employing kingdom authority.

Jesus knew this was necessary for Peter, which is why He sought to comfort him in the midst of His rebuke. We read in Luke 22:32, after Jesus told Simon Peter that Satan had demanded permission to sift him, that "I have prayed for you, that your faith may not fail; and you, when once you have turned again, strengthen your brothers." Even though Satan asked to do a number on Peter and God gave the okay due to Peter's pride, Jesus still prayed for him. He prayed for him to not lose faith. He prayed that when Peter would finally wake up and discover from whom the Source of his strength truly comes, that he would likewise be spiritually prepared to strengthen others going through similar things.

The theological terminology to describe Jesus's prayer for Peter is *intercession*. It is known as the intercessory work of Christ. Hebrews 7 is a foundational passage to explore on Jesus's intercession. We read in verses 23–26,

> The former priests, on the one hand, existed in greater numbers because they were prevented by death from continuing, but Jesus, on the other hand, because He continues forever, holds His priesthood permanently. Therefore He is able also to save forever those who draw near to God through Him, since He always lives to make intercession for them.
>
> For it was fitting for us to have such a high priest, holy, innocent, undefiled, separated from sinners and exalted above the heavens. . . .

For starters, in analyzing the text within the context of this book of Hebrews and this chapter in particular, we know that the audience reading it are Christians. This is important to note because when we read the phrase that Jesus "is able also to save forever those who draw near," we can know He's not talking about saving them for eternity. He's talking about helping them in history. We also can see from this passage that Jesus's help isn't random. It isn't hit or miss. Nor is it whenever He feels like it. In fact, we read that Jesus "always lives to make intercession" for us. From this part of the passage, we know that He is always interceding for us. Not only that, we take confidence in this because Jesus "always lives." This term refers to His resurrection and ascension.

The ascension of Jesus Christ concerns how He died, rose from the dead, and then walked on the earth for forty days. After these forty days, Jesus ascended up to the heavens to sit on the right-hand side of the Father. This is where He now "always lives"—24 hours a day, 7 days a week, and 365 days a year. It is in this position that Jesus intervenes in our situations of life where we need deliverance. It is from this position that He intercedes for us to save us. Remember, though, as we look at this that the "salvation" referenced in Hebrews is not a salvation for heaven. It is saving us from the destruction of the trials and tribulations and temptations on earth.

We can take comfort in this truth knowing that Jesus ever lives to help you and me. In fact, He calls this high calling His priestly duty. The job of the priest in the Old Testament was to serve as a mediator between a sinful people and a Holy God. The way he served as a mediator between sinful people and a holy God was through the sacrificial system. The priest would offer up an animal on a specified day such as the Day of Atonement so that God's judgment against sin would be diverted because of this sacrifice. God's wrath would then be held back so that He could show favor to His people because an acceptable sacrifice had been made.

The sacrificial system was a good system, but it was also a temporary system. It was the layaway plan until Jesus would come and make the payment in full on the cross. Jesus said the word

"Tetelestai" on the cross, which is a word that can be translated to mean "paid in full." This legal transaction completely satisfied the just wrath of a holy God against sinful mankind. In other words, no more payments are needed. No more sacrifices need to take place. Jesus can now "always live" to be the Intercessor on behalf of believers before a Holy God. Because of His intercession, He can act as our legal representative who exercises kingdom authority so we might experience God's favor—help as well as the ability to access, exercise, and transfer His kingdom authority.

Jesus has a full-time job in heaven right now. That is to intercede on our behalf, similar to how He prayed for Simon Peter, but even more so. When Satan comes against you to sift you like wheat, Jesus can intercede in prayer on our behalf, but He also interjects His sacrifice on our behalf. He becomes our advocate in the courtroom of heaven, offering forgiveness and restoration. Not only can He advocate for us from a position of authority, but He can also advocate for us from a position of compassion. We know this based on Hebrews 2:17–18:

> Therefore, He had to be made like His brethren in all things, so that He might become a merciful and faithful high priest in things pertaining to God, to make propitiation for the sins of the people. For since He Himself was tempted in that which He has suffered, He is able to come to the aid of those who are tempted.

Jesus intercedes as a merciful priest. He is a compassionate priest. Jesus knows what it feels like to be tempted because the devil showed up in His own life on earth as well. He understands us better than we realize at times. Which is why He goes to our defense, interceding for us on our behalf in the heavenlies. Hebrews 4:14–16 puts it like this,

> Therefore, since we have a great high priest who has passed through the heavens, Jesus the Son of God, let us hold fast our confession. For we do not have a high priest who cannot sympathize with our weaknesses, but One who has been tempted in all things as we are, yet without sin. Therefore let us draw near with confidence to the throne of grace, so that we may receive mercy and find grace to help in time of need.

You and I have a High Priest who knows what we're going through. That's why He's ready and able to meet you down here whenever you need Him and call on Him up high. Jesus's full-time role is to aid you when you are facing spiritual crises in your life, especially in times of weakness. When Satan is all over you with that addiction, or all over you with that temptation, or all over you with that anxiety, Jesus is sitting at the right-hand side of the Father available to help you. All you have to do is draw near. Keep in mind, to draw near means you can't just be an SMO. That's what I call a Sunday-Morning-Only Christian. If you want Jesus's help and intercession, He wants your heart. Jesus wants a relationship, not religion.

That's why we all must prioritize the pursuit of His presence, through the Word and through abiding with Him. We must come clean before Christ, and recognize our need for His help in our lives. If we choose, instead, to be proud like Peter, we will taste the bitterness of defeat every time. Peter denied Jesus just like Jesus told him he would. Just like Satan lured him into doing, in an attempt to sift Simon Peter like wheat. And after his denial three times, Peter hung his head and cried (Luke 22:62). What's more, he gave up on all he had spent his time investing in with regard to Jesus. He let his failure determine his future, so he returned to fishing (John 21:3).

But that's when Jesus showed up again. That's when Jesus interceded for Peter again. That's when Jesus reminded Peter who He truly was. Peter had lost his hope. He had lost

> When Satan is all over you with that addiction, or all over you with that temptation, or all over you with that anxiety, Jesus is sitting at the right-hand side of the Father available to help you. All you have to do is draw near.

his dream of being a great disciple. He had lost his belief that he could amount to anything in the kingdom of God. So he got back on the boat to fish. Many Christians, like Peter, have put up a "Gone Fishing" sign, having given up hope of ever being restored to kingdom usefulness. But in John 21, we see what happened next. We read of Peter's redemption and return:

But when the day was now breaking, Jesus stood on the beach; yet the disciples did not know that it was Jesus. So Jesus said to them, "Children, you do not have any fish, do you?" They answered Him, "No." And He said to them, "Cast the net on the right-hand side of the boat and you will find a catch." So they cast, and then they were not able to haul it in because of the great number of fish. Therefore that disciple whom Jesus loved said to Peter, "It is the Lord." So when Simon Peter heard that it was the Lord, he put his outer garment on (for he was stripped for work), and threw himself into the sea. (vv. 4–7)

When Peter saw it was Jesus who had come for him, even after he had denied Him three times, Peter jumped into the sea and swam to Him. He didn't even wait, like the other disciples did, for the boat to dock. He just took off for Jesus. Perhaps you know how Peter felt. Perhaps you've blown it once or twice in your life as well. Maybe you've done some things from which you can't see a recovery. You don't see the road to redemption. You wonder how God could forgive you, let alone use you again. But if that's you, I want you to take courage in Peter's story. Because his is the story Jesus wanted him to tell. Jesus had prayed that after Peter was converted from his wrong path of denial, he would strengthen others. He would encourage others in the faith. He would show the way. That's good news. The fact that Jesus knows ahead of time that you may mess things up but that He still prays for kingdom purpose once you repent is good news for all of us. Jesus is the great

Intercessor, who can not only redeem but restore purpose to those who jump in and go to Him.

An interesting thing about Peter's story takes place after Peter had made it back to the shore. I find it interesting because of the uniqueness of the situation. Only two times in Scripture is the word *charcoal* used. Both times in relation to Peter. The first time it is used is when Peter denies Jesus (John 18:17–18). The second time it is used is when Jesus restores Peter (John 21:9). We read:

> Then the slave-girl who kept the door said to Peter, "You are not also one of this man's disciples, are you?" He said, "I am not." Now the slaves and the officers were standing there, having made a charcoal fire, for it was cold and they were warming themselves; and Peter was also with them, standing and warming himself. (John 18:17–18)

> So when they got out on the land, they saw a charcoal fire already laid and fish placed on it, and bread. Jesus said to them, "Bring some of the fish which you have now caught." Simon Peter went up and drew the net to land, full of large fish, a hundred and fifty-three; and although there were so many, the net was not torn. (John 21:9–11)

Jesus took Peter back to the point of his denial in order to call him to a new level of service and commitment. He used a charcoal fire as a symbol of what had happened and a sign of what would come. He used it to demonstrate that Jesus is the greatest in the kingdom of God and it is His power that rules over all. After all, it is His power that can restore even those who have fallen away. Over the smoke of this fire, Jesus spoke to Peter about his purpose. He started by asking Peter if he loved Him. To which Peter replied, "Yes, I do." The question was designed to see if Peter had learned his lesson and dealt with his pride.

But the problem is we can't see Peter's entire reply in the translated text. We have to look at the original language to hear what he said. Because when Jesus asked Peter if he loved Him, He used the word *agape*. Agape love refers to God's sacrificial love, a level of love rooted in commitment. But when Peter replied to Jesus that he loved Him, he used the word *phileo*. Phileo concerns more of a love that refers to friendships and can be situational. Jesus had asked Peter if he had the committed, sacrificial love he had once bragged about before denying him. But Peter had learned his lesson. He knew he could not claim that level of love because he could not back it up with his actions at that time. So he took the love-meter down a notch and said he loved Jesus like a friend.

That's when Jesus gave Peter another chance to claim the commitment he once so smugly stated. He asked Peter again if he "agape'd" Him. To which Peter replied he "phileo'd" Him. Then, in the same number of times as Peter's denial of Christ, Jesus asked a third time. But this time He changed His term. He dumbed down the word. Jesus met Peter where Peter knew he could be at that time. Peter wasn't about to claim a love he might deny. He was too close to his own failure. He remembered the charcoal fire from before and how his love for Jesus didn't mean much at that time—at least not much when it came to Peter's own life. Jesus was using Peter's failure as a teaching tool, showing him the importance of dependency to be successful and prepared for kingdom usefulness (1 Pet. 5:6–7).

So Jesus asked Peter the third time if he loved Him. But this time He asked with the word *phileo*. To which Peter hung his head. He knew what Jesus was doing. He recognized it at that time. We read, "Peter was grieved because He said to him the third time, 'Do you love Me?' And he said to Him, 'Lord, You know all things; You know that I love You.' Jesus said to him, 'Tend My sheep'" (John 21:17). Jesus had met Peter where he was at so He could take him further than he ever dreamed. He can do the same for you and me when we are honest with Him. Jesus doesn't want us to play religious games. He's not easily fooled by our words. Jesus doesn't buy into our bragging. He knows our hearts. And until we, like Peter, also know our hearts and understand our own weaknesses and failures, we will never be able to rely on Christ as our Intercessor. Instead, we will think we can pull things off by ourselves. Which, we can't. You can't. I can't. Only Jesus has the power and the authority to work miracles and greatness both in and through our lives.

I've got good news for you if you feel like you've blown it and don't know how to get back what the enemy has stolen, either through your own spiritual immaturity or sin. God will meet you where you are. He will meet you there as long as you are honest with Him. And when He does that, He puts a block on Satan because now you've gotten right with Him and given Him the legal and relational right to act on your behalf. What's more, He can give you back the years the locusts have stolen (Joel 2:25–26). He knows how to turn things, tweak things, remake things, and restore things. You can get back your dignity. You can get back your destiny. You can get it all back because Jesus knows how to do just that. And He always lives to intercede on your behalf. Come home to Jesus because God is ready to restore you right now. Like a recycling center, God can take what looks useless and has been discarded and remake it for new kingdom usefulness in order for you to fulfill your purpose and exercise kingdom authority for ministry to others. Like Peter, Jesus cannot only restore you, but also gives you a promotion from lambs to sheep (John 21:15–17).

CHAPTER EIGHT

The Alignment

 When my children were small, one of the things I often did was give them piggyback rides. They'd all climb on my back and I would trot them around the den for a ride. I'd like to say I do the same now for my great-grandkids, but the knees won't comply! However, the piggyback ride visual is a great illustration of what it truly means to rest and trust in another. When children climb on the back of their dad, grandpa, or someone else for a piggyback ride, they are allowing their full weight to rest on the other person. They are there in total trust. As a result, they get to experience a fun ride without the cost of waiting outside in a hot line at an amusement park.

Jesus Christ would like to offer each of us something similar. He wants to give you, and me, a piggyback ride. The thing He offers us to climb up on and enjoy is the experience of His kingdom authority. When you and I rest and trust the full weight of our problems, issues, and desires, placing them entirely on Jesus Christ, we get to discover the joy of the journey. We get to realize what it means to piggyback off of His spiritual authority.

The passage that unpacks this for us in greater detail is found in Luke 7:1–10. The story that unfolds in this passage is so powerful that I would like to start off by looking at it in full. It says,

> When He had completed all His discourse in the hearing of the people, He went to Capernaum.
>
> And a centurion's slave, who was highly regarded by him, was sick and about to die. When he heard about Jesus, he sent some Jewish elders asking Him to come and save the life of his slave. When they came to Jesus, they earnestly implored Him, saying, "He is worthy for You to grant this to him; for he loves our nation and it was he who built us our synagogue." Now Jesus started on His way with them; and when He was not far from the house, the centurion sent friends, saying to Him, "Lord, do not trouble Yourself further, for I am not worthy for You to come under my roof; for this reason I did not even consider myself worthy to come to You, but just say the word, and my servant will be healed. For I also am a man placed under authority, with soldiers under me; and I say to this one, 'Go!' and he goes, and to another, 'Come!' and he comes, and to my slave, 'Do this!' and he does it." Now when Jesus heard this, He marveled at him, and turned and said to the crowd that

was following Him, "I say to you, not even in Israel have I found such great faith." When those who had been sent returned to the house, they found the slave in good health.

This account reveals what piggybacking on Jesus's kingdom authority can accomplish in a person's life. The centurion had such great faith in Jesus's ability to heal the person he cared deeply about that he blew even Jesus's mind when he demonstrated his faith. I can say that he blew Jesus's mind because it tells us in verse 9 he made Jesus marvel. It says, ". . . when Jesus heard this, He marveled at him . . ." To make Jesus, the Creator of the universe, marvel is no small feat. But this centurion did just that.

In fact, there exists only one other time in Scripture where Jesus was surprised or shocked—Mark 6:6. Yet this time Jesus's shock had nothing to do with a person's faith. It had to do with the level of the people's doubts. We read, "And He wondered at their unbelief. And He was going around the villages teaching." Jesus couldn't believe that after all He was demonstrating through miracles and healings, that the people witnessing it still couldn't (or wouldn't) believe in Him.

But in the case of the centurion, Jesus marveled at his faith. He called his faith "great." As we will see, the thing that made his great faith was his understanding and utilization of the relationship between authority and alignment. For historical context, a centurion was a mid-level officer in the Roman army who oversaw one hundred soldiers. Each centurion contributed to the overall leadership of a legion, which was made up of 6,000 soldiers. A centurion could be compared to a captain, or possibly a major, in the United States Army.

This particular centurion had a servant who had become ill and was about to die. Word had gotten out about Jesus and what He was doing to heal people. This centurion no doubt had heard that the blind could see, the lame could walk, and the mute could talk. What Jesus had done in miracles and healings had spread far and wide. And while some people still doubted, many others believed. The centurion was one who believed. Seeing that his servant was near death, the centurion made up his mind to go to the healer Jesus and ask for His power of healing to be used for his beloved servant.

Before we get much further into studying his story, though, it's important to realize that just the idea for a Roman to approach a Jew for anything in that day was unheard of. Jews hated the Romans, and the Romans didn't think very highly of the Jews. But this particular Roman man was cut from a different cloth. For whatever reason, this man loved the Jews. We know this because he had spent his own money to build a synagogue for them. He was different. In fact, we saw earlier in the passage that he was known as a man who "loved" the Jews as a nation.

Realizing this, Jesus made a quick decision to head to the man's home to heal his servant. However, before Jesus even got to the house, the centurion sent him a message. He sent Him word that he felt unworthy for Jesus to come under his roof. This man knew himself. He knew his lifestyle. He knew that someone as honorable and pure as Jesus stood head and shoulders over him, even though he was a man of high ranking. He didn't allow his clout or money to confuse him into thinking that he was more than he truly was. This seemingly highfalutin leader in the most dominant global military approached Jesus with a heart of humility. He understood his true place.

Because he knew his place, he also knew Jesus's power. That's why he didn't even need Jesus to come to his home in order to heal his servant. He told Jesus if He just said the word, his servant would be healed. The reason why the centurion could say something like that was because he understood the concept of authority. As a leader in the military, he knew the power of rank. He knew the power of words. He knew what got things accomplished. He knew that if he told someone what to do, the person would go and do it. That's what authority creates. It creates an environment where actions are carried out based on requests, or even demands when given by a legitimate higher authority.

The centurion also understood what it means to live and operate underneath authority too. As a "man under authority," he knew that if his superiors asked anything of him, he had to do it. There was no debate. There was no dialogue. He simply did what they said. That's because authority means exactly that—the authority to decide what takes place.

But what really stood out to Jesus was the centurion used a peculiar word in his statement about being a man under authority. He used the term *also* when referring to Jesus Himself. He said,

"For I am also a man under authority . . ." But Jesus is God. Jesus represents the highest authority of all. And yet this man understood that in Jesus's humanity, He now operated by virtue of His submission and surrender to God the Father. While Jesus is God, He also functions beneath God the Father when it came to authority on earth. We read this more clearly in John 5:19–20:

> Therefore, Jesus answered and was saying to them, "Truly, truly, I say to you, the Son can do nothing of Himself, unless it is something He sees the Father doing; for whatever the Father does, these things the Son also does in like manner. For the Father loves the Son, and shows Him all things that He Himself is doing; and the Father will show Him greater works than these, so that you will marvel."

Everything Jesus did, He did in submission to the Father. And because He submitted entirely to God, He pulled off miracles and actions that caused people to marvel. Living under authority does not mean you limit your ability to fulfill your purpose or do great things. Actually, living under legitimate authority will, more often than not, free you up to do greater things than you would have on your own; that is, if the authority you live under and surrender to is a legitimate authority, such as God. The reason why Jesus was able to be over so many things such as disease, sickness, and demons while He walked on earth was because He was underneath God's authority in heaven. He was over because He was under. The centurion understood that. He knew what authority could do, and that's why he appealed to Jesus's experience with authority Himself, by saying the word *also*.

The principle for each of us as we live our lives today is that in order to gain access to the miraculous, you must live out your days underneath the legitimate kingdom authority of God. You cannot exercise legitimate authority over what you are supposed to be over unless you learn to operate *underneath* that which God has placed over you. If you choose to rebel against what God has legitimately placed over you, then you will not receive heaven's help to carry out the kingdom authority you have over what is under you. This is an example of living out of spiritual alignment.

Alignment is a key feature of the way God operates in history. When we are out of spiritual alignment, we are in contempt of court since God is a God of order (1 Cor. 14:33). When angels rebelled against divine order, they were judged (Jude 6). When Satan got mankind to rebel against God's divine order, they were judged (Gen. 3:1–24). Alignment and kingdom authority go hand in hand.

Rebellion hurts you more than anyone else, if it is rebellion against legitimate spiritual authority. We see this play out in our everyday lives when people rebel against legitimate human authority.

I like to illustrate the power of authority through the use of football. Authority is about a system of who is in charge. It is not about who has the most strength, or even smarts. For example, in football, the referees are in charge. The players may be younger,

stronger, and faster while the referees are older, slower, and fatter—
but the players must yield to the referees. All the referees need to
do is blow their whistles or throw their flags to shut down whatever
might be taking place on the field. Now, the reason why these older
and slower referees have the right to overrule the faster, younger,
and even stronger guys is due to the system of authority established
by the NFL. That system delegates authority to the refs. Because
the referees are underneath the NFL's authority and rules, they are
over the NFL players and what happens on the field.

That's how delegated authority works. That's why whatever
legitimate authority that has been placed over you by God should
be honored. It is in honoring the authority over you that you gain
greater freedom and power to exercise all you were created to be on
the field of life. The point is that you cannot exercise authority over
something until and unless you are submitted under the legitimate
authority that is over you. And because most people do not understand this theological principle, their prayers do not get answered.
Their victories do not get achieved. Their power does not get recognized. And the changes they desire to take place in their lives
don't occur simply because they are operating out of alignment
with regard to the legitimate authority God has allowed over them.
Once you are misaligned in God's kingdom program, you have cut
the cord of the transfer of spiritual authority to and through your
life.

The centurion understood this principle and, truthfully, he
didn't need Jesus to come to his house in order to heal his servant.

All he needed was for Jesus to say the word and his servant would be healed.

The Bible makes it clear that Satan is operationally under the believer's feet (Rom. 16:20). Now, that does not mean Satan is always situationally or circumstantially under the believer's feet, because when a believer fails to access and use kingdom authority, Satan cleverly deceives them to think he has more power than he does. But according to the Scriptures, Satan *is* underneath the believer's feet. We read this in Romans 16:19–20:

> For the report of your obedience has reached to all; therefore I am rejoicing over you, but I want you to be wise in what is good and innocent in what is evil. The God of peace will soon crush Satan under your feet.
>
> The grace of our Lord Jesus be with you.

To be *under foot* means "to be underneath the authority" (Josh. 10:24). It does not mean literally underneath the physical feet of believers but symbolically, spiritually, and operationally. Satan holds no legitimate authority over any follower of Jesus Christ. Any authority he taps into and uses is based on deception. We can see this one verse earlier in Romans 16:18:

> For such men are slaves, not of our Lord Christ but of their own appetites; and by their smooth and flattering speech they deceive the hearts of the unsuspecting.

Satan's strength lies in his ability to deceive. Because if a believer lives his or her life based on the truth of God's Word, then Satan will not be effective in carrying out his schemes against them. It is only through deception that Satan gains the higher ground.

Now, if you are thinking the authority belongs to Christ alone—based on the passage we read in Romans—I want to point out this same power and authority that Jesus possessed while on earth was transferred to His followers. We discover this in Luke 9:1–2:

> And He called the twelve together, and gave them power and authority over all the demons and to heal diseases. And He sent them out to proclaim the kingdom of God and to perform healing.

Jesus gave the power and authority the disciples needed to cast out demons and heal diseases. Similarly, when we trust in Christ as our Lord and Savior, He can give us the same level of kingdom power and authority to fulfill His will. Many of us have things that are trying to overpower us. We face demons and demonic activity seeking to trip us up. Satan would love to own you, control you, and dictate your emotions. But because Jesus has legitimately given you access to His kingdom power and authority, Satan does not have the last say. Satan does not have the upper hand. He does not stand on higher ground. You do. But it's up to you to recognize that truth so you can internalize it so you can flesh it out in your day-to-day experiences.

Jesus has told us clearly, "All authority has been given to Me in heaven and on earth" (Matt. 28:18). All authority. Thus, since Jesus has all authority, He has the authority to delegate this authority to whomever He chooses. This is why our alignment to Jesus Christ spiritually as His kingdom disciples is so critical. If you want heaven to join you in history and heaven's authority to overpower that which opposes you on earth, you must be comprehensively aligned beneath the Lord Jesus Christ (Rom. 14:8–9). Alignment with a specific church won't cut it. Alignment with a specific denomination won't cut it. It's only when you are rightly aligned to Jesus Christ that you tap into the kingdom authority that is His to give out.

The issue of alignment is essential because that is how authority flows. The centurion demonstrated his understanding of this concept by asking Jesus simply to say the words of healing over his servant. He knew Jesus held the authority over sicknesses on earth so all He had to do was command the sickness to be gone for it to be gone. Much of the confusion we experience today in our relationships and situations falls into one category as the source: misalignment. When believers try to live lives out from under the proper alignment beneath the Lord Jesus Christ, all

> If you want heaven to join you in history and heaven's authority to overpower that which opposes you on earth, you must be comprehensively aligned beneath the Lord Jesus Christ.

sorts of issues arise. If you are out of alignment, whatever you seek to pull off either won't work or it won't last.

Have you ever experienced what happens to a car when the tires are out of alignment? Things get shaky real fast. When the car is out of alignment, the wear on the tires will become uneven and cause the ride to be less than ideal, even intolerable at times.

> Spiritual victory is rooted in spiritual alignment.

Our lives are not much different than our cars, in this regard. If and when we are out of alignment with the rightful authority of Christ over us, our lives will wear out unevenly. Things will get shaky, bumpy, and less than ideal. What we aim to do either won't come about or it won't remain if it does come about. Spiritual victory is rooted in spiritual alignment (1 Cor. 11:3).

Colossians 3:17–25 breaks down this area of alignment into certain categories for us. Let's read it in full and then look at the different aspects of alignment it covers:

> Whatever you do in word or deed, do all in the name of the Lord Jesus, giving thanks through Him to God the Father.
>
> Wives, be subject to your husbands, as is fitting in the Lord. Husbands, love your wives and do not be embittered against them. Children, be obedient to your parents in all things, for this is well-pleasing to the Lord. Fathers, do not exasperate your children, so that they will not lose heart.

Slaves, in all things obey those who are your masters on earth, not with external service, as those who merely please men, but with sincerity of heart, fearing the Lord. Whatever you do, do your work heartily, as for the Lord rather than for men, knowing that from the Lord you will receive the reward of the inheritance. It is the Lord Christ whom you serve. For he who does wrong will receive the consequences of the wrong which he has done, and that without partiality.

In these verses we can identify the key elements of alignment. It begins with every single one of us choosing to do all things as to God Himself. Each of us is called to be in alignment underneath God. It starts there. If and when we fail to live underneath God, then everything else underneath us is subject to the consequences of misalignment as well.

Next, the flow of alignment extends to wives who are to live their lives being subject to their husbands. Now, this refers to the legitimate authority as a husband. If a husband is not living all of his life in alignment underneath God (the first principle in this passage), then he cannot expect his wife to align underneath him. Areas of his spiritual rebellion can cause her to compromise her commitment to Christ. Otherwise, she will also be misaligned under God. But wives, if your husband is seeking to live his life underneath the authority of Christ, then it is your responsibility to align yourself underneath him. If you choose not to do that, then you are similarly choosing not to align underneath God's authority because authority has a flow to it. This will, then, limit your access to divine, spiritual authority in your own life.

In the next section of the passage, we read that husbands are to love their wives and not be embittered against them. This principle means that men are not to be disrespectful or dishonoring to their wives in any way. There is no room for abusive—whether verbal, psychological, or physical—behavior. Nor is there an allowance for neglectful behavior. Husbands must be careful not to be obstinate nor dismissive to their wives. To love a woman is to actively, righteously, and compassionately seek her well-being, even above your own.

After detailing the flow of authority and the husband's role in the home, Paul tells us in the next verse that children are to be obedient to their parents in all ways. The reason why parents are to teach their children to obey is not just because you want them to mind. The reason you teach them to obey is because it brings great joy to God. Their obedience pleases God. And when God is pleased, He often responds with answered prayer. This is due to the prayers being offered up while in submission to His overarching authority.

In fact, when Paul writes of this in his book of Ephesians, he explains that the obedience of children will enable them to live long on the earth. God will so honor them coming under His legitimate authority as outlined by their parents that He will guard and protect them. This doesn't imply that no one will ever die young. But what it does mean is that when children live in obedience to their parents who are aligned under God's rule, they will not die early. They will not leave this earth ahead of the divinely prescribed time.

Next, the passage outlines for us the role of parents with regard to alignment under authority. Fathers are told in verse 21 not to exasperate their children, otherwise the children will lose heart. It's interesting that the verse is specifically addressed to fathers. This is similar to Ephesians 6:4, which says, "Fathers, do not provoke your children to anger, but bring them up in the discipline and instruction of the Lord." In biblical times, it was a normal part of cultural understanding that the fathers were responsible for raising their children. Unfortunately, this has drifted from the norm in society today—most children today are raised primarily by their mothers.

But men have a high calling when it comes to raising children. Men are responsible for the spiritual imprint of their children. They are responsible for the discipline of their children. Your wife is there to help, but the ultimate responsibility falls on your shoulders. If and when a man fails to fill these shoes with regard to his children, he is operating out of alignment from God's prescribed way. We read an example of a man being called to fulfill this responsibility in Genesis 18:19:

> "For I have chosen him, so that he may command his children and his household after him to keep the way of the LORD by doing righteousness and justice, so that the LORD may bring upon Abraham what He has spoken about him."

We live in a day of male abandonment in the areas of responsibility men have been given. We see this in the homes. We also see this in the churches. Unfortunately, we also see the consequences of this misalignment in our homes, churches, and society. Men must live out their God-ordained responsibilities if we are to experience an improvement in our culture.

Following children, Paul lets us know we are to all be aligned underneath whomever it is we serve at work. The passage says we are to carry out our work not merely to please men, but we are to do it with a sincerity in our hearts because we fear God. We are not called to whistle while we work; we are called to *worship* while we work. Everything we do is to be done to the glory of God because it is Jesus Christ whom we serve—not your boss, supervisor, or any entity under which you serve.

You ought to look at your job as a role to please the Lord. When you do, it will not only affect your attitude, but it will also impact your productivity. When you know that Jesus rewards hard work and commitment to His values of excellence, integrity, and service, then it makes it easy to work well. Jesus has His own incentive program and you tap into it by working underneath His authority and for His glory.

Paul finishes out this look at authority and service in Colossians 4:1, which speaks to those who oversee others with regard to work. He calls each of us in roles like these to a management style based on justice and fairness. The reason why we are to conduct our lives in this way is because we too have One who is over us in heaven. This is why it is important to treat everyone fairly and with kindness.

In addition, God calls church members to submit to the legitimate authority of their spiritual leaders (Heb. 13:17). And citizens are to submit to the legitimate authority of their political leaders (1 Pet. 2:13–15).

When life is lived out underneath the prescribed authority structures God has set up, it will run more smoothly. You will experience what it is like to have answered prayer. You will know how to use your spiritual authority. If you really want to witness heaven do things that will blow your mind, then learn to live all of your life in alignment underneath His authority.

The centurion's servant was dying, and yet when Jesus saw the faith of the centurion who asked Him to heal his servant, He gave him what he had requested. In fact, Jesus so marveled at the centurion's faith that He even turned to the crowd who had gathered and said, "I say to you, not even in Israel have I found such great faith" (Luke 7:9). Essentially, Jesus was calling out His own people. In today's terms, we might say He threw them under the bus. He was letting the Israelites know that He had not found such great faith as this centurion had, even among His own people. Again, the key to his faith was his understanding of the relationship of alignment to spiritual authority.

Jesus rewarded the centurion's great faith by doing what he asked. He healed his servant. We see in verse 10 that when the people returned to the house where the once-sick servant had been, they now found him in good health. His healing came about immediately. What's more, Jesus didn't even have to go there and see him, or touch him, or do anything to him in order to heal him. Jesus's spiritual authority rules over all, whether He is right there or not. And once you understand this truth, you can align yourself underneath Him in such a way so you can tap into His spiritual authority to overcome whatever has come against you.

As we go through this book together, I want to challenge you to go for a piggyback ride. I want to challenge you to take Jesus seriously with your faith by aligning under His kingdom authority and reflecting His rule in the things He has placed under your charge. He wants you to do just that. He wants you to climb up onto His back and ride on this kingdom authority principle. If you are living out of alignment from God's rightful rule over you, then make the effort to get into alignment right now. Surrender to God and His authoritative rule over you. When you do that, you will begin to access the kingdom authority you need in order to live out your divine purpose. You can walk with your head held high as you walk as a victor and no longer a victim, all due to your spiritual alignment under God as well as all the spiritual authority that alignment allows you to access.

CHAPTER NINE

The Thorn

 To enjoy the fragrance of perfume, you've got to break the sealant holding the perfume inside. To enjoy chewing a peanut, you've got to break the shell so the nut can emerge for you to eat it. For a butterfly to take flight, it must break the cocoon so it can rise to its intended level of flight. And for Christ to take each of us to our next level of spiritual growth, He has to break us of our self-sufficiency. This is because self-sufficiency, contrary to how it may seem, actually holds a person back. There is little that God dislikes more in a believer's life than self-sufficiency. This is because self-sufficiency is often rooted in pride; it gives an individual the thought or feeling they can function independently of God.

Wherever self-sufficiency exists, pride often exists as well. Thus, in an effort to truly develop us to live out the full realization of our divine purposes and kingdom authority, God will often bring about a breaking. He will allow a cracking to occur in order to help rid His followers of their feelings of independence. One of the chief ways God strips us of this independence and self-sufficiency is through His use of the devil. See, the devil is not just the devil. The devil is God's devil in that God will often allow the devil to carry out a work that He knows will bring about a greater good in the individual. The devil has to get permission from God to do what he does with regard to believers covered underneath God's covenant.

God rules so comprehensively and completely that even hell is at His command. Hell can also operate at times of His choosing according to His intended purposes. The devil and his demons have to function when God gives permission to them. Sometimes this involves situations God uses to humble us or increase our awareness for dependence on Him. We read about one of these situations in 2 Corinthians 12, where Paul, the author of this letter to the church at Corinth, has just come out of a spiritually elevating experience. If you'll read through the first six verses of that chapter, you'll see that what Paul went through would blow anyone's mind. He got to visit the "third heaven." In fact, Paul is the only human being who has gotten to visit heaven in that way and lived to come back and talk about it. He said he saw things that were unlawful even to utter. He didn't have the words to describe what he saw because words did not exist in our languages that would be sufficient.

Paul saw unimaginable glory, greatness, and truth. He witnessed a reality no one else has witnessed while walking the earth, apart from Jesus Christ, and, no surprises here, he potentially experienced an increase in his own personal self-worth and pride. To put it in everyday terms, Paul could have gotten the big head because he realized he was specially chosen to experience what no human had ever experienced before.

That historic context helps explain what Paul writes in 2 Corinthians 12:7, which says, "Because of the surpassing greatness of the revelations, for this reason, to keep me from exalting myself, there was given me a thorn in the flesh, a messenger of Satan to torment me—to keep me from exalting myself." Because God had allowed Paul to go higher than any human being had ever been before, He knew there would be the propensity toward pride. He knew Paul would be inclined to think more highly of himself than he ought to think. So, to counter that, God allowed something in his life to remind him that the privilege He had given to Paul was not Paul's own attainment. It was a gift from God, through grace.

I wonder if anyone reading these pages and beginning to experience a greater level of spiritual authority and spiritual success in your life has ever been tempted to think more highly of yourself than you ought? Maybe God has blessed you with more money than you thought you'd ever have. Maybe you drive a new car. Or you live in a very comfortable home. Maybe you've got degree letters after your name that set you apart from the crowd. Or maybe you've witnessed God's kingdom authority overturn and overcome people and situations in your life that cause you to marvel. Whatever the case may be, it's easy to think more highly of ourselves when we are swimming in blessings and even experiencing spiritual prosperity. But, as Scripture says, "Pride goes before destruction, and a haughty spirit before stumbling" (Prov. 16:18).

God opposes the presence of pride in our lives because God knows the source of our blessings and greatness. He is the source. As James 1:17 tells us, "Every good thing given and every perfect gift is from above, coming down from the Father of lights, with whom there is no variation or shifting shadow." God is the source of good in our lives, and He takes offense when we confuse that with our own pride and self-sufficiency.

The most celebrated day in my life was also the worst day in my life. In November of 2019, our national ministry, The Urban Alternative, along with my four kids, put on a celebration at the local church where I pastor, Oak Cliff Bible Fellowship. This celebration came about because I had become the first African American to write a study Bible and full Bible commentary in history. We celebrated that night with music, festivities, fellowship, and special guests. It was wonderful. But, on the same night, my wife of forty-nine years had to be helped down the aisle just to walk to her seat because she was dying of cancer. Seeing her barely able to make it to her seat, and knowing how much energy she had sought to reserve in the weeks preceding the event so that she could attend, broke me.

Here I was celebrating a lifetime achievement with this unique accomplishment that I had poured countless hours into producing, all the while crying at the same time. I had no temptation to think more highly of myself than I ought as I watched with utter help-lessness as my wife's life ebbed away before my eyes. And, to be honest, God keeps that picture in the front of my mind as a way of reminding me I may have been given the privilege of prospering in my service to Him, but I was unable to do the one thing I wanted to do most—save my wife. That reality will remove pride each and every time.

God will give a great grace to anyone who is humble. But He actively opposes any level of pride that pops up in His servants (James 4:6–8). He may have given you opportunities and privileges to serve Him, and these privileges may have even ushered in your recognition and a greater level of social significance. But, because He loves you, He will make sure you do not forget where your tal-ents, ideas, time, resources, and energy ultimately come from. It is all sourced in Him. Even, your kingdom authority.

That's why I have chosen to define kingdom authority like I have. It is not something that we create in and of ourselves. Kingdom authority is a delegated authority to us. Without God creating it, backing it, and delegating it—we cannot use it. As a reminder, kingdom authority can be defined as *the divinely autho-rized right and responsibility delegated to believers to act on God's behalf in spiritually ruling over His creation under the lordship of Jesus Christ.*

Following Paul's experience in the third heaven, Paul could have easily exalted himself in his own mind. He could have mistakenly begun to believe that the kingdom authority he both witnessed and carried out was rooted in his own piety or skills. That's why God gave Paul a "thorn"—a "messenger of Satan" sent to humble him and put him in his place. Keep in mind, Paul doesn't tell us exactly what this thorn is, and that's probably so we don't fixate on the thorn itself, but rather on the principle behind it as well as apply it to our own unique thorns. This thorn could have been a physical ailment, a sinful lust, or even a thorny person in his life. No doubt Paul faced them all in some form or fashion (Gal. 4:12–15; Rom. 7:14–25; 2 Cor. 7:10).

> Kingdom authority is a delegated authority to us. Without God creating it, backing it, and delegating it, we cannot use it.

Whatever the thorn was—and it's possible it took different shapes or different forms over time—it nagged him nearly to death. It drove him nuts. It tormented him and created a misery in his existence that was unable to be dismissed or ignored. Paul recognized that this pain had a purpose to it. That's why he referred to it as a "messenger of Satan" and stated that it was even given to him to accomplish something significant in his life. This wisdom allowed Paul to identify the problem for what it was: to allow the purpose of the problem to bear fruit in his life. Paul knew there was a heavenly reason for this hellish invasion in his life, and that reason involved preventing him from exalting himself too high.

A spiritual principle that applies to all of us but it is often so easy to ignore is that the higher you are to go in serving God, the lower you've got to go with God. The more you want to hear from God, the more humble you've got to be before God. If you get all puffed up before God, He will send Satan to humble you. He does this to remind you that you have limitations, and your Source for all you do and accomplish for good in this life is Him. Every breath you take is from Him.

There are many ways God seeks to humble us. Sometimes it involves problems and issues with our finances. Other times it could be health issues. Sometimes it involves people in our lives who irritate us, or even insult us, as Paul said they did to him. Whatever it is God uses to humble you, though, you will recognize it as something you cannot ignore. You can't get away from it on your own. It'll be an irritant that can feel like a prison until you discover the lesson hidden within it. God loves you so much that He does not want to see you waste your life on pride. He felt the same way for Paul.

That's why when Paul asked God to remove the thorn from his life three separate times, begging God for relief, God refused. He allowed the thorn to remain because the thorn had a purpose it needed to produce. In Paul's situation, the purpose was to let Paul know that God's grace was sufficient. It was to let Paul know that he ought not exalt himself. It was to let Paul know that all things

> The more you want to hear from God, the more humble you've got to be before God.

really do work together for good for those who love God and are called by Him (Rom. 8:28). Let's read more in depth on Paul's situation in 2 Corinthians 12:8–9:

> Concerning this I implored the Lord three times that it might leave me. And He has said to me, "My grace is sufficient for you, for power is perfected in weakness."

When God gives you a thorn for your spiritual benefit, even if the thorn is provided by the devil, it's to keep you in a position where you can exercise kingdom authority. Because if you exalt yourself with pride, you will no longer be able to carry out the spiritual authority that comes through a humble alignment underneath God's rule. Kingdom authority rests in a right relationship to God. Pride disrupts that relationship. Recognizing this ought to help shed light and broaden your perspective on why God will allow, or has allowed, seemingly negative situations and painful scenarios in your life.

Ladies who own pearls as part of your jewelry collection probably understand already how pearls are formed. Pearls are created through pain. Essentially, an oyster or clam gets a grain of sand in it and it becomes an irritant. This irritant could be described as a thorn in the flesh. When the grain of sand gets lodged in the oyster or clam, its membranes become so irritated that they try to get rid of it. Yet because the grain of sand is so deeply embedded, it simply cannot get rid of it. So what it does is then secrete something around it so the irritant no longer has access to its tender skin. This secretion hardens over time, and that is what becomes a beautiful pearl.

Paul teaches us through his own example that if we allow the secretion of God's grace to surround whatever it is that is irritating us in our lives, this grace will turn what was once something awful into now something beautiful and valuable. Coating life's irritants with grace, which is God's unmerited favor, produces new life and new strength within the hearts and minds of believers.

The most potent verse on grace is found in 2 Corinthians 9:8. It is one of my favorite verses, and it is a key principle to remember as you navigate life. I encourage you to commit it to memory. It says, "And God is able to make all grace abound to you, so that always having all sufficiency in everything, you may have an abundance for every good deed . . ." Grace is so sufficient that it can cover every situation you face. In fact, when you allow the free flow of God's grace to produce fruit in your life, you will have an abundance of all you need to carry out every good deed you can. God can always create something valuable in our lives when we commit it to Him with a heart of humility. Like a woman who is pregnant and in labor, the weakness and pain is birthing something good. Grace mixed with pain equals power.

Yet Paul only became aware of this benefit of grace when he asked God to remove the thorn from his life. God does not always answer our prayers as we want. Paul wanted the thorn removed. But God responded with grace that was sufficient to handle the thorn. God may not change your situation when you come to Him in prayer, but He will give you a greater grace with which to face it and find the good being produced through it. God's grace is sufficient.

If you are reading this book and you have a situation that has not changed, or an illness that has not healed, or a job difficulty that has not been reversed, a financial challenge you have not been able to meet, or a relationship that has not been restored—and you have prayed for God's intervention—then know that He is giving you the grace sufficient to it. I want to remind you to open your ears, eyes, and your heart to hear and learn what God is doing through the pain He is allowing in your life. That may mean turning off the television at night so you can spend dedicated time in His presence. That may mean reading your Bible more than you do right now. That may mean stilling the thoughts in your mind so you can focus on God's still, small voice with which He will often speak. Because if God hasn't fixed the scenario you've asked Him to fix, then He has a purpose for prolonging it. God is always intentional.

> If God hasn't fixed the scenario you've asked Him to fix, then He has a purpose for prolonging it. God is always intentional.

Paul gives us insight into how we are to respond to painful situations in our life in such a way that will produce the greatest outcome. We read this in 2 Corinthians 12:9b–10, "Most gladly, therefore, I will rather boast about my weaknesses, so that the power of Christ may dwell in me.

Therefore I am well content with weaknesses, with insults, with distresses, with persecutions, with difficulties, for Christ's sake; for when I am weak, then I am strong."

Did you catch that? Paul said he would brag about his weakness. He opted for bragging about his insufficiencies rather than his gifts such as going into the third heavens. Now, don't confuse this with telling the details of every issue you face over and over again. That can actually keep you stuck in a mental loop where you don't find a productive way to face your issues. God is not calling us to be masochistic or to make ourselves feel miserable. No, Paul said he would brag about his weaknesses so that the light of God's grace could shine even more brightly.

When Paul found out God was using the devil to make him a better Christian, he decided to cooperate with the circumstances. He didn't resort to blaming. He didn't play the victim card. He became wise to the point of realizing that God had a great plan for him and the pain was part of that process. The reason he chose to brag was because in pointing out what God was doing, it opened the door for the power of Christ to dwell in him. He opened the flow of a greater grace, thus receiving a greater power, as well as greater access to kingdom authority than he had before.

A fundamental way Paul opened up this flow of grace was through the practice of contentment. He said he had become content with his weaknesses, and even with his distresses and difficulties. To be content with something means to be at rest with it on the inside, regardless of the circumstances on the outside. It has to do with a calming peace internally, which is rooted in an acceptance of God's sovereign plan. Paul demonstrates contentment for us in Philippians 4:10–13:

> But I rejoiced in the Lord greatly, that now at last you have revived your concern for me; indeed, you were concerned before, but you lacked opportunity. Not that I speak from want, for I have learned to be content in whatever circumstances I am. I know how to get along with humble means, and I also know how to live in prosperity; in any and every circumstance I have learned the secret of being filled and going hungry, both of having abundance and suffering need. I can do all things through Him who strengthens me.

Paul tells us in this passage that contentment is a learned trait. It's not natural to us. We don't possess an automatic response mechanism of contentment, but it is a virtue that can be learned. In fact, it is a virtue that should be learned and applied because life is not all sunshine and candy. I wish that I could tell you if you would just follow Jesus all of your problems would go away, all the money you want would come to you, and you would gain access to your greatest wish. I wish I could give you fake news when it comes to following Christ because that would make my job easier and all of our lives easier too. But that's not how reality works. Neither is that how spiritual growth works. Rather, as we've seen far too often in our culture today, giving someone everything he or she wants leads to a spirit of entitlement and narcissism. Those two things produce destruction in the paths of all who come into contact with them.

God is interested in producing good and growth in our lives, so difficulties do arise. We learn to grow in our walk with Him when we discover the secret of contentment. The reason Paul was able to be content was because he had changed his perspective on pain. He had changed his perspective on problems. In recognizing God's grace and His sovereign plan, Paul realized God will often use pain to produce something greater on the other side of it. If and when God doesn't give you the solution to whatever problems you face, if you are truly asking Him to do so or to provide wisdom in the midst of it, He will give you sufficiency. He will give you grace. He will give you the power of contentment, which then produces a wellspring of peace within you.

How do you know when you have reached a spiritual level of contentment? You can identify that you have arrived at this level when you are more thankful than you are complaining. When you feel gratitude more than you grumble, you are unleashing the power of contentment in your life. Contentment is the key to unlocking spiritual authority because contentment provides the internal atmosphere for abiding and worship. Contentment recognizes that there is one God, and you are not Him. It allows room for God to move and work wonders behind the scenes, even when everything you can see doesn't seem to make sense.

If you are facing a challenge right now, I want to encourage you to go to God in prayer. Be honest with Him. Tell Him you are hurting. Tell Him you are disappointed. Tell Him whatever it is you are dealing with doesn't make sense to you. But then after you have told Him all of this, ask for His wisdom and grace. Ask Him to show you the power that is greater than your weaknesses so you can find the strength to go on.

In my home, we have power strips situated throughout the various room. The reason why we plugged in the power strips so many years ago is because a normal wall plug only has two outlets, but we may need to plug in three or four different things at once. Contentment is like a power strip in a Christian's life. It opens the flow of grace so you can handle more, do more, glorify God more, and experience His spiritual power more. Contentment positions you to receive the full force of God's kingdom authority into your life and move through you to others as you remain rightly aligned underneath His overarching rule.

> When you feel gratitude more than you grumble, you are unleashing the power of contentment in your life.

CHAPTER TEN

The Truth[1]

 The supreme authority that a king holds over his subjects by virtue of his office, the Bible holds by virtue of its Author, who is the King of creation and thus Ruler over all the earth. The Bible's authority is inherent in its every word and even every portion of a word. The Bible is also supremely authoritative because it is God's revelation in history.

When I say the Bible is God's voice in print, I mean that the words of Scripture come from His mouth. I want to use the term "God's voice" here to help you grasp what we might call the immediacy of the Bible's authority. That is, the Bible's authority is timeless. For example, when we read in Exodus 20:3, "You shall have no other gods before Me," this command has the very same force behind it today that it had when God first thundered these words to Moses more than three thousand years ago. This is important;

one problem I see as a pastor is that people disregard God's Word because to them, it's just informal or inspirational ink on a page, thus limiting the experience of God's authority in their lives.

Receiving the Bible as God's voice speaking directly to us is important because of another common problem among God's people. This shows up when people know what God said, and can even repeat it back to you, but they aren't doing anything about it. Every parent is familiar with this scenario. Your child disregards your direct instructions, and when you confront that child later and ask, "What did I tell you to do?" he or she can repeat your words verbatim. But for some reason your command didn't carry any weight with that child, so the result was disobedience. And a good parent won't let that go without appropriate discipline (Heb. 12:5–6).

God *has* spoken to us in His Word. He has told us what to do, how to think, and how to live. Scripture is God's voice in print. So, when we live our lives according to the Bible, we need to do so according to the authoritative nature of His Word, applying the truths from the Word to our thoughts and decisions so we can experience and exercise spiritual authority.

Jesus was being challenged by His opponents one day when He tried to tell them that He was God. They objected, accused Him of blasphemy, and got ready to stone Him (John 10:31–33). Jesus turned to the Scripture to make His case, and the way He used the Word has a lot to teach us about the Bible's authority:

Jesus answered them, "Has it not been written in your Law, 'I said, you are gods'? If he called them gods, to whom the word of God came (*and the Scripture cannot be broken*), do you say of Him, whom the Father sanctified and sent into the world, 'You are blaspheming,' because I said, 'I am the Son of God'?" (vv. 34–36, emphasis added)

Jesus was using a powerful argument here. He said that if the Bible—in this case the psalmist Asaph (Ps. 82:6)—used the term *gods* for men who were merely God's representatives, then those who were accusing Jesus should not object if He called Himself God. Why? Because they had just seen Him heal a blind man (John 9) and do other miracles.

What I want you to see here is the binding authority of Scripture. Not even one word can be changed. Scripture is irrefragable, which means it cannot be voided, canceled, or invalidated. How important is this trait? It was important enough to Jesus that He built a critical argument around it. Scripture is the foundation for kingdom authority.

The Lord's opponents might have wished they could nullify or get around the word *gods* in Psalm 82:6, because it is the Hebrew word *Elohim*, which is one of the names of God. But Jesus had them, because God's Word called His representatives "gods," and nothing could change the Scripture.

Paul used a similar tactic in Galatians 3 to prove that Jesus is Abraham's promised seed. The validity of Paul's entire point hung on the difference between the singular "seed" and the plural "seeds"

(v. 16). Not only each letter of the Bible, but even the smallest part of each letter (Matt. 5:18), is vital and carries God's authority.

Jesus Christ also said the Bible carries the imprint of His divine authority. He announced to His disciples, "Heaven and earth will pass away, but My words will not pass away" (Matt. 24:35). That statement on the lips of anyone other than Jesus would be heresy, but He alone can claim, "All authority has been given to Me in heaven and on earth" (Matt. 28:18). Therefore, Jesus's words, which are recorded in Scripture, will outlast history, because the Word is eternal. I love the way the psalmist put it: "Forever, O LORD, Your word is settled in heaven" (Ps. 119:89).

Now, I don't know about you, but this raises a question in my mind. Since Jesus possesses all authority, and His Word has all of His authority behind it, why are we as followers of Jesus Christ not seeing God's Word at work? I am convinced the reason is that far too many of us are failing to live as though God's Word were our authority, which limits or denies us of the experience of exercising kingdom authority. We are not seeing more power in our lives because we aren't taking the Bible seriously.

The fact that the Bible is completely authoritative and cannot be broken or canceled is a wonderful doctrine of the Christian faith. But the truth and power of God's Word can be nullified in your experience if you refuse to let the Word speak to you as it is or you start mixing it up with your human viewpoints.

Now please notice I did not say the Bible can lose its power or authority. That will never happen because God said His Word is "forever settled in heaven." But the Bible's power is blunted in our lives when we do not respond to God in humility and obedience to His authoritative Word.

This is probably the number one travesty that people who claim to believe and follow God's Word commit against it. A lot of people who try to mix their own thoughts with the Bible's teaching have many degrees after their name. Education is fine, and the church has benefited from well-trained commentators and scholars who seek to understand what the Word means. This is not what I'm talking about. There's a big difference between an honest attempt to understand the Bible as it reads and diluting its teachings with human thinking. The best example of this is in Scripture itself, when the Pharisees and scribes came to Jesus to accuse His disciples of breaking "the tradition of the elders" (Matt. 15:1–2).

But Jesus came back at them with a much more serious charge—that of nullifying the Word of God (vv. 4–6), using the example of God's commandment to honor one's father and mother. Jesus showed how the scribes and Pharisees allowed people, mainly themselves, to get around this clear command with a hollow promise to give those resources to God while actually not having to give them away at all.

Jesus gave the bottom line of this kind of thinking when He said at the end of verse 6, "And by this you invalidated the word of God for the sake of your tradition." The point is that God never meant for the commandment to honor your father and mother to be skirted on a technicality.

The Jews added so many traditions and regulations to the Law that they ended up creating a barrier around the Word so people couldn't get to it. The Bible says, "Let God be found true, though every man be found a liar" (Rom. 3:4). The issue Jesus dealt with was the authority of God's Word. If God says we are to honor our parents, then trying to find a "loophole" in that command is a sin against the truth.

This thing of truth and authority is at the core of why the Holy Spirit is not exercising more kingdom authority in and through our lives. The Spirit is the Spirit of truth who is obligated only to God's Word. So when we start diluting the Word with our human viewpoints, the Spirit steps back, because He is not going to bless or empower our speculations.

There's an interesting story in 2 Kings 4:38–41 about the prophet Elisha and the "apprentice prophets" who were under his tutelage. There was a famine in the land, and these student prophets were hungry. Elisha told his servant to make a pot of stew for everybody, and one of the prophets gathered some wild gourds for the stew. The gourds looked fine to him, and he probably thought they would add a little spice to the stew. He decided to help out by tossing the gourds into the stew.

But as everyone ate, some apparently began to feel sick and said the stew was poisoned. Someone cried out to Elisha, "O man of God, there is death in the pot" (v. 40). Elisha added substance to the problem, and the stew was fine.

Unfortunately, this happens every Sunday in churches all across this nation. Plenty of pastors and teachers are tossing "wild gourds" into the pot—adding human wisdom to God's Word or even allowing human views and opinions to replace the Scriptures. This is why people can actually be worse off by going to church, because they come away more confused and unsure than ever about whether the Bible is even true, let alone whether it has any relevance to them. A mist in the pulpit creates a fog in the pew.

Biblical kingdom authority means staying true to God's truth alone. It also means that God has the supreme right to determine our decision-making and set the agenda for our lives. God doesn't want our rationalizations. He wants our response to His Word.

Keep in mind, it doesn't matter whether you agree with it or disagree with it; Scripture is still true. It is the absolute standard by which reality is to be measured. It doesn't matter whether you like it or don't like it; Scripture is still true. It doesn't even matter whether you want it or don't want it. It remains irrefragable on all accounts. Scripture can never be rendered as non-authoritative. Either you will choose to receive the Scripture as completely reliable and trustworthy, or else it will simply look like a collection of inspiring words. That distinction is very important in carrying out spiritual authority in your life.

> Biblical kingdom authority means staying true to God's truth alone.

Either you believe that the Bible represents words about God or you know it to be the authoritative Word *of* God. If you believe it to be words about God, then they are just nice words to hear and be encouraged by. They lift you up and make you feel better. But if that's all you get from the Bible, you're not getting all it was created to give. God does not simply want to give you inspiration from His Word. He wants you to experience the authority of His Word as you activate its work in your life through obedience (James 1:22–25). Scripture is His authority in print. It is the Word of God Himself.

The reason why I have confidence in prophecy and can speak about things to come is because I'm not just talking about my own thoughts or beliefs. I am speaking about the Word of God. Scripture has God's stamp of authority on it. The Bible is the living voice of God in print (Heb. 4:12–13; 2 Tim. 3:16–17).

The Bible is not merely a nice book you read every once in a while in order to have a verse a day to keep the devil away. Scripture is the infallible, inerrant voice of God. If you are a person who desires to hear from God or desires that God would speak to you, then you should be in your Bible every day. The Bible is His voice. When you read Scripture, God will often personalize a passage to your situation, but you will never know or understand this if you are not there reading it.

You can actually hear God's voice if you are willing to recognize it with your spiritual eyes and ears. In other words, His internal witness will always be collaborating His external record,

Scripture, which cannot be broken or undone. In fact, the Bible will break you long before you break it. Everybody who has ever tried to destroy it has been destroyed by it first. Every culture that has banned it has died or diminished in influence before the Bible died. That's because it cannot be broken. God's voice will not be negated. Jesus rested His authority on it and in it. We are to tap into His kingdom authority by studying and applying the truth of God's Word. But that is very hard for many people to do, as we see in the earlier example of Jesus with the Jews. In John 10:17–20, we read even more context to the passage that opened up this chapter:

> "For this reason the Father loves Me, because I lay down My life so that I may take it again. No one has taken it away from Me, but I lay it down on My own initiative. I have authority to lay it down, and I have authority to take it up again. This commandment I received from My Father."
>
> A division occurred again among the Jews because of these words. Many of them were saying, "He has a demon and is insane. Why do you listen to Him?"

The Jews were calling the One who could cast out demons a demoniac Himself. After all, Jesus claimed to forgive sins. He could make the blind see. And He had no issue in declaring He was One with God Himself. But the Jews didn't have room for that in their belief constructs. They chose to invalidate Jesus's claim even though Jesus used the Scripture as a basis to back it. Scripture cannot be broken. It is authoritative. Jesus argued that His authority as the Son of God was based on Scripture itself.

Matthew 24:35 states, "Heaven and earth will pass away, but My words will not pass away." What God is saying in that passage is that Scripture will outlast history itself. It cannot be broken or canceled (John 10:35). I am convinced one of the reasons we are not seeing more kingdom authority made real in people's lives is because we are failing to take the Scripture seriously. The Bible possesses all inherent authority. When we use it merely for inspiration, we are not tapping into divine authority.

Jesus's words are authoritative in nature. You can either accept them or reject them. Just like when Jesus turned the water into wine in John 2, the individuals had to act on His Word as authoritative and do what He said, or they could choose to ignore it. To ignore, or reject, the authority of Scripture is to reject Christ. You can't love Jesus and not give deference to the authority of His Word. This is because His words have authority. People have opinions. Jesus has authority. The Bible will actually lose its operational authority in your life and experience when you infuse it with your human viewpoint. Now, it never loses its authoritative power or validity, but it does lose its operational authority in your life.

The Bible records an amazing story in Jeremiah 36, an attempt made by King Jehoiakim of Judah to destroy God's message that the prophet Jeremiah had recorded on a scroll. The king cut up the scroll and burned it (vv. 22–23), but God simply told Jeremiah to get another scroll and write His Word on it again.

The eighteenth-century French philosopher Voltaire despised the Christian church and boasted that within fifty years of his death, Christianity would be extinct and people would have to go to a museum to see a Bible. Yet after Voltaire died, his house in France was acquired by a Bible society and used to print and distribute Bibles.[2]

God says His Word will stand forever (see Ps. 119:89; Isa. 40:8). There is no destroying the Bible, because it is the eternal Word of God comprised of the essential truths we all need in order to align our lives under God's governing rule.

A college professor stood up before his class one day and said, "I want to begin this philosophy class by getting to the bottom line with a statement that will govern everything we study and talk about this semester. The bottom line of this philosophy class is that there are no absolutes. There is no such thing as absolute truth, no propositions that are true in every circumstance. Let me say it again. The bottom line of this philosophy class is that there are no absolutes."

A student in the back raised his hand and said, "Professor, may I ask a question?"

"Yes."

"You said there is no such thing as absolutes, and no such thing as a statement of absolute truth. Are you absolutely sure about that? Because if you are, you have just given us a statement of an absolute that is true in every circumstance, which is a contradiction of the assertion you just made that there are no absolutes."

That exchange may sound like the kind of academic double-talk that makes parents wonder what in the world their children are learning in college and why they have to pay so much for it. But the student who challenged his professor made a very important and valid point about the issue of truth, and about the absurdity and contradictions people get themselves into when they try to deny the existence of a concept called truth.

How would you react to a doctor who was unsure of his diagnosis of your condition, but gave you a prescription anyway, which you took to a pharmacist who wasn't even sure he was giving you the medicine the doctor had hesitantly prescribed? You would probably run for your life from both of them, since your health and life might be at stake. You want to go to a doctor and pharmacist who believe in truth, a fixed standard of reality that guides their decisions.

The problem is that many people who insist on living by truth in the physical realm confidently reject it in the spiritual realm. But simply announcing that truth does not exist does not solve anything. We are faced with this thing called truth, and we have to do something with it.

Pontius Pilate asked the question of the ages when truth Incarnate in the Person of Jesus Christ stood before him on trial. Jesus said to Pilate, "For this I have been born, and for this I have come into the world, to testify to the truth. Everyone who is of the truth hears My voice" (John 18:37).

Pilate responded, "What is truth?" (v. 38).

If that evil Roman governor had been an honest seeker, he would have found the answer to his question. In fact, Jesus had definitively answered Pilate's question the night before at the Last Supper, during His prayer to the Father on our behalf: "Sanctify them in the truth; Your word is truth" (John 17:17). The Bible is truth—the whole truth and nothing but the truth. It is therefore the source and basis for the understanding and exercise of kingdom authority. Yet, rejecting Scripture's authority cancels our exercise of kingdom authority.

The world has always been confused and divided on the question of truth. There have been a myriad responses to the question, "What is truth?" The *denier*, for lack of a better term, is the person who simply dismisses and rejects the very concept of truth.

The agnostic says that absolute knowledge on issues such as God's existence cannot be attained in this life. Since the word *agnostic* literally means "without knowledge," the agnostic's answer to Pilate's question would be "I don't know." This person is supposedly the perpetual questioner and seeker after truth.

The rationalist says that human reason and experience are the ultimate criteria for determining truth. *Rationalism* focuses on the mind and simply says that whatever the mind conceives of as being reality is, in fact, truth. Rationalism thus limits the search for truth. It is one of the theories that came into play during the eighteenth-century movement known as the Enlightenment, when the truths upon which Christianity is based came under sustained attack and were largely abandoned.

There is also a school of thought called *positivism*, which says truth is limited to what can be validated by the scientific method. If science authenticates a theory, then perhaps we can regard it as truth. Positivism doesn't leave any room for a supernatural Savior with a supernatural revelation, because these things cannot be reduced to the scientific method of testing something and repeating it time and again in the lab until its reality can be established.

Another of mankind's many answers to the question of truth is *fideism*, which reacted to the rationalistic and scientific method by saying that truth is subjective and personal. Truth is what we feel at the moment to be true, so therefore what's true for me may not be true for you.

Pragmatism is yet another means of seeking to arrive at truth. Pragmatism appeals to a lot of people because it says that truth is whatever works. This kind of approach is tailor-made for our American love of "my truth" thinking that says we are each entitled to our own version of truth.

I need to mention one other significant route people have taken to try and arrive at truth. This is man-made religion, defined as humanity's best attempts to reach up to and understand God—or even deny that He exists or cares about what happens to us. The *religionist* may be the hardest person of all to deal with, because he's the person who claims to be a follower of God and a seeker after spiritual truth. But more often than not, religion begins by denying the absolute truth that God has spoken with finality in Jesus Christ (Heb. 1:1–2).

I am not saying that people cannot discover certain truths on their own. But the problem with the world's "truth" is that it often has to be revised or discarded when new facts are uncovered. Hundreds of years ago, people were convinced the earth was flat. It was feared that if explorers sailed to the edge of the earth, they might fall off. But that "truth" had to be discarded when new evidence was found.

How about a contemporary example of changing truth? If you follow the world of nutrition and health today, your head is probably spinning trying to keep up with all of the new, and sometimes conflicting, information about the content and value of certain foods.

Since research is constantly going on, today's facts may be tomorrow's myths. There seems to be no final word there. And we can't trust our moral instincts to determine truth, because we have been corrupted by sin. Our intellect is also a poor guide to truth, because we are finite creatures whose knowledge is extremely limited.

The only reason we can know any truths at all is that God is God. Truth is not just that which conforms to reality, because there is no reality apart from God. Truth is that which conforms to His nature. We as Christians can make an unapologetic, uncompromising, definitive statement about truth because of the perfectly true nature of God. The Bible calls God the Father "Him who is true" (1 John 5:20), and Jesus made the astounding statement, "I am the way, and the *truth*, and the life" (John 14:6, emphasis added).

Here's one example of the way God's nature is the standard for what is true. The Bible says, "God is not a man, that He should lie" (Num. 23:19). Lying is wrong not just because it messes people up and causes harm, but because it violates God's very nature. The same can be said for murder and theft and adultery and coveting. These things are out of line with God's character. Truth and purity are part of His eternal attributes.

So while the world says truth is whatever we want to make it, God says truth must conform to a fixed standard. If I gave you a sheet of paper and a pencil and asked you to draw a straight line freehand, no matter how meticulous you were, your line would not be perfectly straight. But if I gave you a ruler with a sharp edge to draw your line against, the outcome would be totally different. As long as your pencil follows that fixed standard, your line will be straight. And anyone else can take that same ruler and make a straight line too. Since God is by nature true, something must conform to Him and His written revelation to be true.

> Truth is not just that which conforms to reality, because there is no reality apart from God. Truth is that which conforms to His nature.

God safeguarded the truth of His Word through the process called divine inspiration. As we looked at earlier, the apostle Peter, who experienced this inspiration, said the Holy Spirit oversaw the writing of Scripture so there was no contamination in it (2 Pet. 1:20–21). This is why we can say that God is the Bible's true Author, thus giving Scripture divine authority that allows us, then, to exercise kingdom authority.

But even though the Bible's human authors were "moved" or "carried along" by the Holy Spirit, they often appealed to their own experiences and witness as reliable. Peter said, "We did not follow cleverly devised tales when we made known to you the power and coming of our Lord Jesus Christ, but we were eyewitnesses of His majesty" (2 Pet. 1:16). Peter went on to relate the transfiguration of Jesus, which Peter saw and heard (vv. 17–18). John, another apostolic eyewitness, wrote about "what we have heard" and "what we have seen with our eyes" (1 John 1:1).

The writers of Scripture were safeguarded from error by the Holy Spirit, who moved them to write and bore them along in the process. These men were so convinced of the truth that they were willing to die for it—which is a strong argument for the Bible's truth, by the way.

Let me tell you, even if I was part of a conspiracy to say that Jesus was the Son of God and had risen from the dead when I knew it was a lie, when people said they were going to kill me, I'd be showing them where the body was, but the writers of Scripture stood by the Word even when it meant their deaths.

It is important to hold these truths close to your heart and mind based on the authoritative nature of Scripture. The Bible is the complete truth, and the theological term that refers to that is the word *inerrant,* which means "without error." In its most basic form, inerrancy means that God's Word forms an absolutely fixed, firm foundation of perfect truth. Some people will say the Bible contains truth or contains the Word of God. But that's only half the truth, because it leaves open the possibility that the Bible also contains other things. The inerrancy of Scripture means the Bible is true no matter what the subject. And because it is true, it carries the ultimate authority over all things. As you come to study and memorize and apply scriptural truths, you will discover you are accessing and utilizing kingdom authority without even trying. It will come naturally as a result of the power of God's Word at work in and through you.

CHAPTER ELEVEN

The Testimony

 Whenever a person faces a medical challenge that won't go away, or where over-the-counter remedies don't seem to work, the doctor will order tests to dig deeper. The doctor needs to conduct a professional analysis of your crisis so that he or she can determine your cure. Inevitably, the physician will order scans such as MRIs or X-rays. These allow him or her to look beneath the surface of the issues causing you pain, struggle, and stress. The point is to peek beneath what is seen in order to uncover the problem so that a treatment can be applied.

The subject of kingdom authority often requires us to look beneath the surface of what is taking place in our lives. If we are to address the issues and chaos in our emotions, relationships, and circumstances, we have to first identify what is giving rise to them.

What exists beneath the surface—in the unseen spiritual realm—that is producing such upheaval in the physical?

Jesus had to do the same when He walked the earth. In Mark 5, we read of an electric story where this took place. The story tells of a man who was demonically oppressed. We often refer to this man as the demoniac. The entire first half of the chapter focuses on this man gone wild. We're told that when Jesus had been traveling and He had gotten out of the boat, having crossed the Sea of Galilee, that He came to a man from the tombs. What that means is the man lived like a homeless man. He lived in a graveyard and among the tombs. He didn't live in the vicinity of life. He lived in the vicinity of death. His comfort zone equated to being surrounded by that which no longer lived. That was his home.

Not only did he live among the tombs, he also lived in a state of crazed behavior. He had become out of control. No one was even able to bind him anymore, not even with a chain. This man's demonic possession had become so entrenched that his strength overpowered the powers that be. No one could calm the chaos he caused.

Because he had been bound with shackles and chains, and he actually tore apart the chains, people feared him. He was screaming among the tombs and gashing himself with stones. He had resorted to self-harm in unimaginable ways. Satan and his demons want nothing more than to deceive and influence people to harm themselves. When that takes place, the demons don't even have to do the harming themselves. That's the greatest form of destruction in a person's life, and it happens all the time.

But this specific man's situation was more graphic than most. Perhaps God included his story in Scripture so we could all learn from it since it is so stark of an illustration. But self-harm and isolation take place in much more subtle ways, yet can be as equally devastating. Whether it's giving in to a propensity to overeat (comfort food), binge entertainment, be sexually promiscuous, drink to get drunk, overspend, or sabotage work or social relationships—wherever self-harm takes place, the damage is often at dangerous levels.

This man's life story reveals to us in graphic terms what it looks like to be out of control. Our human terminology for him would be something like "crazy" or a "sociopath." Many people today would say he needs to be put away in an asylum. Some would even have him arrested. According to Luke 8:27, he walked around nude. We read, "And when He came out onto the land, He was met by a man from the city who was possessed with demons; and who had not put on any clothing for a long time, and was not living in a house, but in the tombs." In contemporary culture, he would have been locked up for indecent exposure. His situation was sheer madness.

But Jesus didn't stop at assessing the surface of this man's life. He knew there was more to the story. While most would label what he suffered from as mental illness, Jesus knew there was more than that taking place.

Unfortunately, our American culture is suffering from a mental health crisis. And while some of it truly is a result of mental illness,

I would argue that a lot also has to do with demonic possession or demonic influence. We have, as a society, opened ourselves up to demons in so many ways.

In Mark 5:2, we see what was causing this man's world to run into the ground. He had become controlled by an unseen hand. He was being informed and defined by a demon. There was something deeper going on in this man's life than just mental instability. We read the entire story set up in verses 1–5:

> They came to the other side of the sea, into the country of the Gerasenes. When He got out of the boat, immediately a man from the tombs with an unclean spirit met Him, and he had his dwelling among the tombs. And no one was able to bind him anymore, even with a chain; because he had often been bound with shackles and chains, and the chains had been torn apart by him and the shackles broken in pieces, and no one was strong enough to subdue him. Constantly, night and day, he was screaming among the tombs and in the mountains, and gashing himself with stones.

This passage reveals a lot. First, we see he was clearly possessed. It says he was a man with "an unclean spirit." Next, we discover he was very powerful—"no one was strong enough to subdue him." Lastly, we notice he is in tremendous emotional and physical pain. This man spent his days and nights "screaming." I do want to emphasize again before we get much further that *not all mental illness is tied to demonic possession.* There are a multitude of causes, so my intention is not to heap condemnation on someone struggling through mental illness. Instead, I do want to raise our attention to the spiritual battle happening in the unseen realm, where there is certainly a battle for our hearts and minds. While there exists mental illness that comes about through chemical imbalances or biological abnormalities needing to be addressed, there also exists mental illness rooted in demonic influence, oppression, or even possession. We're specifically told in this situation the man's actions were controlled by an unclean spirit. "Unclean" is another way to speak of unrighteous. This man had unaddressed unrighteousness running rampant in his life.

One thing to do when examining a situation or person who has a pattern of being out of control is to examine whether or not there are spiritual issues that have gone unresolved. If you fail to do that, you may be seeking to address a problem through an over-the-counter solution that won't truly fix the issue at hand. Medicine cannot cure a sickness derived from a spiritual causation. Whenever there exists unresolved sin issues—unrighteousness—in the life of a person, it will become a welcome mat for demons. Like trash left to rot attracts roaches and rats, sin left unaddressed attracts demonic activity and influence. You don't have to give a formal invitation to a roach, rat, or mouse in order to draw them in. All you have to do is let trash sit too long in your home, garage, or yard. You never have to advertise for flies to set up camp and produce maggots. All you have to do is let trash rot long enough and you'll have maggots soon enough. The right conditions draw them in. Similarly, a sinful soul with unaddressed unrighteousness will draw in demons—whether through demonic influence, oppression, or possession.

Whenever someone refuses to address the unrighteousness within them, that person has participated in their own demise through allowing demonic influences to increase over time. What that person has done in inviting demonic attention to an unclean situation is helped to make a bad thing worse.

Have you ever sought to get rid of an infestation of roaches or flies by only killing the roaches or flies? If it's an infestation, there is a reason why. Something has been left to rot that has drawn them in. You can kill the roaches and flies all day long, but if the thing that was left to rot that has drawn them in is not removed, you'll just wind up with new roaches and flies in the place of those you've killed. The area must be cleaned so the roaches and flies stay away for good. If you have a problem with roaches, stepping on one roach at a time won't solve it. You need to call in the exterminator who will look beneath the surface to find out what is causing the infestation as well as spray to remove the entire group of roaches—not just one.

Much of the chaos we are witnessing in our culture with people losing their minds is not just that they are criminal, mean, or don't care about others. Rather, many of these individuals have been demonized. The unresolved issues and sin in their lives leaves us weak, and like a lion pounces on its weakling prey, Satan can use our vulnerable position against us. Solving the social issues being promoted and exacerbated by those under demonic influence won't happen by merely stepping on the symptoms. We must go beneath the surface to identify and address the cause if we are ever to see lasting improvement in the overall mental health in our land.

Just a few minutes watching the news or scrolling through social media will tell anyone we live in a culture gone mad. We live in a society where numerous people simply do not care about life anymore, or its value. We live in a country where many people do not care about property or preserving it. Many people have lost all sense of decorum and respect in how they speak to each other. We are no longer shocked to hear about or witness abuse—whether verbal or other. It's not that people have lost their minds. Rather, by and large, it is because people have allowed their minds, souls, and bodies to be influenced, oppressed, or even possessed by demons from the pit of hell.

Now, before you start to puff yourself up with pride in thinking that because you are a Christian, you could never yield to demonic influence in any way, I want to remind you *everyone* is susceptible. Christians may not be able to be possessed because we have the Spirit dwelling in us, but Christians can still partake in demonic activity and open ourselves up to being influenced or oppressed by demons. Don't just take my word for it, take Paul's. In writing to Christians at Corinth, he got onto them for taking part in demonic activities. He wrote in 1 Corinthians 10:18–20,

> Look at the nation Israel; are not those who eat the sacrifices sharers in the altar? What do I mean then? That a

thing sacrificed to idols is anything, or that an idol is anything? No, but I say that the things which the Gentiles sacrifice, they sacrifice to demons and not to God; and I do not want you to become sharers in demons.

Paul warned the believers not to "become sharers in demons." Thus we see from this passage that even Christians can fellowship with demons. As a result, there are certain things that we can't seem to get rid of in our lives, family relationships, or in our addictions because demons have attached themselves to them. Demons have amped them up. Demons have weaponized them against you. You are no longer just fighting an issue or a problem, you're fighting the demonization of the issue or problem. That's a whole different battle, and a whole different level of strength to go up against. If you recall from the earlier passage about the man with the unclean spirit, his strength overpowered anyone who tried to chain him down. Demons are strong. Humanity does not possess the strength to defeat them on our own. That's why understanding, accessing, and applying Christ's kingdom authority is so critical.

Not only are demons strong, they are also clever. We see in 1 Timothy 4:1–5 that they come with a lot of false information. Paul calls them "doctrines of demons." They twist things, distort things, make evil sound good and good sound evil. These demons even know how to talk sweetly and enticingly to draw in the weak-minded and entrap them under their demonic influence. Their information is always contrary to the truth and knowledge of God, but they will often make it sound as if it is the truth and what God has to say is a lie.

What must be considered anytime a person's life, or your own in any way, is being ruled by something illegitimate, is whether or not the root of the issue is deeper than what the surface may initially reveal. It needs to be discerned whether there exists inflammation in the soul due to demons that have been invited into the uncleanliness of the environment. As we see with the example of the man living in the tombs, his issues were ongoing. Mark 5:5 says he struggled both "night and day." His was a lifestyle, not just a moment, of pain and suffering,

That is one indicator of whether demonic influences have made themselves dominant. If the issues remain cyclical and continual—meaning, as soon as one issue is solved, another one pops up and the pain seems to be on a loop—then it could be demonic influence. If it's something that just won't seem to go away no matter what you try and you can't seem to defeat it, then you need to know it could be demonic at its root. It's often demons who have attached themselves to addictions that keep the craving and addiction cycle on repeat. Willpower never defeated a demon. Only the power of Jesus and His Word can do that.

Look what happened in verses 6–7 when Jesus entered the scene of the demoniac: "Seeing Jesus from a distance, he ran up and bowed down before Him; and shouting with a loud voice, he said, 'What business do we have with each other, Jesus, Son of the Most High God? I implore You by God, do not torment me!'"

The man controlled by demons literally had his demons drag him to Jesus's feet and kneel down because Jesus was tormenting the demons. Jesus had been telling the demons to come out. "For He had been saying to him, 'Come out of the man, you unclean spirit!'" (v. 8). The demons knew the power and authority of Jesus. They knew they held no ground if He were to command them to come out. So, they literally ran and bowed before Him to beg Him not to torment them. That's how much power Jesus has. That's called kingdom authority when even the demons have to bow. I use the plural form of demons because we see in verse 9 that when Jesus asked for a name, He got this reply: "And he said to Him, 'My name is Legion; for we are many.'"

A whole herd of demons had taken residence in this man. No wonder he was messed up. But that's what demons will do. They will distort a person's view of himself or herself to such a degree that all they are left with is confusion. They no longer know who they are. Many people have demonized tongues which is why they feel the need to swear or cuss all the time. Many men have demonized fists, which is why they wind up being abusive to their mates. Many people suffer from demonized attitudes about themselves, which is why they can openly live as racists or elitists or bullies. Anytime demons are given a foothold, they'll try to creep in for more. Before you know, "legion" has taken root.

Legion. A Roman legion was 6,000 soldiers. When the demons referred to themselves as "legion," they acknowledged their numbers. This man had roughly 6,000 demons in him. We shouldn't find that too unusual because demons tend to congregate. They run in crowds. The wilder a person gets or the more chaotic and evil he or she becomes, the more demons are setting up camp. In fact, we're living in a culture today where people have not only been demonized but entire societies have been demonized. As 1 John 5:19 says, "The whole world lies in the power of the evil one." Entertainment, politics, sports. Almost all of the aspects of our lives have been swayed by his influence in one way or another. Various aspects of society at large have allowed demonic influence, oppression, and even possession to infiltrate and take over their realms.

A few years ago I had an infestation of bees that had set up camp in our house. They would literally come into our home in hordes. So I did what anyone would do; I called the professionals to come and get rid of the bees, which they did. The problem was that the bees would be gone for a while, but in no time at all, they would be right back. They liked to congregate in our bathroom, so before you knew it, the bathroom would be buzzing once again. I got stung more times than I want to count.

Over time the professionals discovered the bees had built a nest in our attic. They wound up in the bathroom because they had made a way from the attic to the cooler air of the bathroom below. But even though the professionals would go into the attic to get the bees up there, they still managed to show up again. One group of professionals even located the hive and got rid of it. But in less than a month later, the bees were back in our bathroom.

You can imagine how I felt calling the bee removers back for the umpteenth time telling them I literally had dozens of bees in my bathroom. No matter what they tried, the bees just kept coming back. After enough attempts to get rid of them, I decided to go with someone else. So, I called another company and told them about my problem. As I was explaining how long this problem with the bee infestation had been going on, the man said in a very matter-of-fact voice, "The reason why your problem is not solved, Tony, is because you are asking the wrong question."

"Excuse me?" I replied.

He continued, "You're asking the wrong question. That's why you can't get a permanent solution."

"Okay," I said, growing impatient. "What is the question I should be asking? School me."

He said, "You've been starting at the wrong place. In order for them to build a nest in your attic, they have to be able to get into your house. And because you have not identified the source of their entry into your house to build their hive, removing the hive does no good at all. When you get rid of it, all they have to do is come back in and rebuild it."

The previous company had been trying to manage my problem rather than identify a permanent solution. They had identified the pathway from the attic to the bathroom. They had also identified the hive in the attic. But they had not identified a pathway from outside the house into the attic. As a result, the bee infestation lasted far longer than it ever should have. It wasn't until the new exterminator took a walk around the outside of my home that he was able to identify the source of the infestation.

There was a small hole on the side of my house that had been allowing the bees access. The exterminator pointed to the hole and said, "This is your problem. When you solve this, you solve that problem inside." When he had closed the access to the interior of our home, and removed the hive once again from the attic, he solved the problem for good.

That experience reminded me of how demons can keep coming back. If you don't solve the problem at the point of entry, you won't solve the problem of demonic influence. Removing one here or there won't cut it in the long run. They'll just move back in and start influencing you all over again. That's why dealing with the root of an addiction or a harmful thought pattern or negative attitude or any issue in your life must be done at the source of the problem. If you focus solely on the symptoms, you will never address the source. Unfortunately, far too many of our behavior-modification programs or self-help books deal with symptoms. But no 12-step program can kick a legion of demons out once they've set up a camp and fortified their entrance. Only Jesus can do that.

Which is exactly what Jesus set out to do with the demoniac. He told them to come out. But when He did, they became afraid. They began to beg. In fact, they even implored Him:

And he began to implore Him earnestly not to send them out of the country. Now there was a large herd of swine feeding nearby on the mountain. The demons implored

Him, saying, "Send us into the swine so that we may enter them." Jesus gave them permission. And coming out, the unclean spirits entered the swine; and the herd rushed down the steep bank into the sea, about two thousand of them; and they were drowned in the sea. (Mark 5:10–13)

The demons were being tormented. They were being asked to leave the man who had become their home. At that point, the most they could do was beg for help. They implored Jesus not to torment them any longer. You may have heard when a person is a drug addict or an alcoholic and they want to get free, they want to let go of the craving that has them bound, they will often check into a facility or go into a room where they become tethered for a period of time. The reason for the tethering is to help hold them in place when their body goes through "withdrawals." The body can physically sweat, shake, and tremble violently, so the tethering is to keep them safe.

If you have ever experienced this yourself, if you know someone who has, or if you have witnessed it on a show or program, you have an idea of the level of torment that takes place. In order to become whole and healed, the person first passes through excruciating pain. He or she goes through a period of discontinuity where things are not flowing in concert with one another. But there is a willingness to go through this because the person wants the evil off their back. In order to be rid of the evil, things often have to get worse before they get better.

A similar thing happened with the demoniac. The demons created all sorts of increased pain and chaos as they feared for Jesus using His kingdom authority to cast them out. They sought for another place to reside. This is because they needed a host to transfer into. Since pigs were considered unclean animals to the Jews, they identified the pigs as a host that Jesus might agree to send them into.

Jesus granted their request, and once the demons took up residency in the pigs, they rushed down the steep bank into the sea and drowned. This illustrates for us a primary goal for demons—death and destruction. That is why much of what is behind suicidal tendencies or actions can be traced to demonic activity or influence in a person's life. Demons drive people to depression in hopes they will become self-destructive, even to the point of committing suicide.

When word got out about Jesus's power over the demons, and how the demons had entered into the swine that then drowned in the sea, the people in the city and also in the country began to implore Jesus to leave their area (vv. 16–17). They had seen the former demon-possessed man now clothed and in his right mind. But that didn't give them cause to celebrate Jesus. Instead, they focused on the destruction of the herd of pigs and became afraid of Jesus's power and authority. So they asked Him to leave.

Rooted within their reasons of asking Jesus to leave is because the people in that region made their money off of the pigs, but their business model had been interrupted. Their economics had sunk. Their lifestyle would take a hit while Jesus healed the lifestyle of the man who had once been bound. They obviously didn't see this as a good trade-off. This is a similar reason that Jesus gets kicked to the curb in our culture today. His values and His power run contrary to many of the business models that profit off of the poor, the sick, and the addicted. Jesus heals. Jesus empowers. Jesus lifts up. Jesus drives out the demons.

This is one reason why many forms of government such as socialism and communism attempt to dumb down or get rid of religion altogether. Faith in the kingdom authority of a Higher Being can cancel out or reduce the profitability of their systems. These leaders want man-made mandates instead of God-ordained values instructing societal ways. Jesus gives strength to the weary and a greater grace to those who need it most.

This is why it's no surprise that the former demoniac asked to go with Jesus when He was about to leave that region. This man knew His power and wanted to stay near Him (v. 18). But Jesus didn't let him. Instead, He instructed him, "Go home to your people and report to them what great things the Lord has done for you, and how He had mercy on you" (v. 19). So the man went on his way. We read in the next verse that he "began to proclaim in Decapolis what great things Jesus had done for him; and everyone was amazed" (v. 20).

The "Decapolis" is a ten-city region. The man didn't just go home to his town or village and tell what had happened. Rather, he became a traveling evangelist sharing the good news of Jesus Christ to all who would listen. His example is a good example for all of us. When Jesus has restored you or healed you or redeemed your life from the pit, don't forget to tell others about it. Don't just use His kingdom authority for your benefit without sharing the good news of that authority with others. His authority isn't just about you and for you. It is a message of spiritual liberation everyone needs to hear and gain access to.

Wherever you go, make it a point to tell what Jesus has done for you so He can continue to work through you to deliver others as well. That's the point of kingdom authority made manifest in your life. It is designed to lift and empower followers of Jesus Christ not just locally, but worldwide. I want to challenge you as you read this book to make your testimony public. Whatever Christ has done for you or is about to do for you, be sure to take your testimony beyond the church walls. Encourage others with what He has done so they can also grow in their faith and draw closer to Jesus and His authority in their lives as well. Let your life be a testimony and conduit of what kingdom authority looks like in someone who you bring to Jesus for the power of God's kingdom authority to operate in their lives.

CHAPTER TWELVE

The Return

 We all have appliances in our homes, predominantly in our kitchens. These appliances have been manufactured for a purpose. Refrigerators keep things cold. The stove cooks things. The toaster allows the bread to get heated and crispy. Whatever the appliance may be, it has been manufactured with an intended purpose in mind.

When appliances are working properly, they serve their intended purpose. But we all know that appliances sometimes break down. There comes a point where they are no longer living up to their created purpose or the expectations of the owners. When that time comes, it's important to have a warranty. A warranty allows you to contact someone who is sufficiently equipped and authorized to fix what has been broken at little or no cost to you.

As we've seen throughout this book, Satan's priority is to derail you from your purpose. His goal, and the goal of his demons, is to disrupt your life at such a level that you are broken, beat down, and unable to carry out the destiny God created you to fulfill. Jesus came to give life. Satan came to destroy dreams, hopes, joy, and ultimately to even take your life before the intended time. You cannot defeat Satan and experience spiritual authority simply through positive thoughts and affirmations. Nor can you defeat Satan through your own strategies. The only way to defeat Satan's deceptive power in your life is through the authority of the shed blood of Jesus Christ. It is kingdom authority that exists as your warranty to get what has been broken—be it emotionally, physically, spiritually, relationally, or any other—working once again.

> The only way to defeat Satan's deceptive power in your life is through the authority of the shed blood of Jesus Christ. It is kingdom authority that exists as your warranty to get what has been broken—be it emotionally, physically, spiritually, relationally, or any other—working once again.

If you want to reclaim what the enemy has stolen and fix what the devil has broken in your life and situations, you need to approach the devil fully using the kingdom authority found in Christ. You must defeat Satan legally with legitimate spiritual authority. You can't outwit him. You won't outlast him. And you certainly can't outplay him. But what you can do is tap into the authority of the One who can do all of that, and more. The kingdom authority of Jesus Christ gives you and me the ability to take back what the enemy has stolen and prevent Satan and his demons from continuing to be grifters in our lives.

As we wrap our time together on this topic, I want to focus on how to apply this principle of spiritual authority in such a way that you maximize your time on earth. Let's start by looking at Zechariah 3. This biblical account takes place in a heavenly courtroom. We have a judge, a prosecuting attorney, and a defense attorney present. We also have a defendant. Let's read verses 1–5:

> Then he showed me Joshua the high priest standing before the angel of the LORD, and Satan standing at his right hand to accuse him. The LORD said to Satan, "The LORD rebuke you, Satan! Indeed, the LORD who has chosen Jerusalem rebuke you! Is this not a brand plucked from the fire?" Now Joshua was clothed with filthy garments and standing before the angel. He spoke and said to those who were standing before him, saying, "Remove the filthy garments from him." Again he said to him, "See, I have taken your iniquity away from you and will clothe you with festal robes." Then I said, "Let them put a clean turban on his head." So they put a clean turban on his head and clothed him with garments, while the angel of the LORD was standing by.

I want you to notice that Joshua was standing in dirty clothes. This indicates his position in life at that time. It tells us a lot about what he was facing and how he may have even been feeling. His accuser, Satan, stood before him hurling all forms of insults and accusations, as a prosecuting attorney, against him. Because of the southern kingdom of Israel's rebellion against God, they were facing judgment by being taken into captivity by Babylon. After seventy years in Babylon, they were in the process of being restored to Jerusalem. Joshua was one of the priests. Part of his duties was to facilitate this restoration process. He does this through guiding the spiritual direction for the people.

Knowing how critical of a kingdom purpose this is, Satan has chosen to pluck Joshua from the fire to bring him before God for accusation. Satan wants to get rid of him because he doesn't want Joshua to leverage kingdom influence for the benefit of God's bigger purpose—the restoration of Jerusalem. Satan knows if he can cut Joshua off at the knees so he can no longer perform his duties, he can halt the larger plan of kingdom deliverance, redemption, and restoration.

When Satan comes against you, like he came against Joshua, it is important to recognize he may be coming against you to halt a larger plan. You have a kingdom part to play. God created you to fulfill a divinely designed destiny. Part of thwarting that destiny involves tripping you up. Satan wants to steal the dreams, goals, and hopes that you have because in doing so, he also strips you of your contribution to a greater collective kingdom purpose as well.

For Joshua, it meant stopping him from the ultimate restoration of Israel from whom Jesus would one day come. So, to prevent that from taking place, Satan took Joshua to heavenly court. In court, he accused him of his "filthy garments." These garments symbolized a sinful lifestyle that had in some way engulfed him. Even though he was a spiritual leader and a high priest, he was now dressed in unrighteousness. We know it is unrighteousness because in verse 4 of the passage we looked at earlier, we read it was his "iniquity" that was taken away. Iniquity is sin. Not only was Joshua clothed in filthy garments outwardly, we know he was polluted with some form of sinfulness on the inside.

Satan probably assumed he had the goods on Joshua. He thought his accusations would stick. He had legal rights to take Joshua before God and point out his unholy lifestyle. He wanted to remove Joshua from his place of leadership based on legitimate concerns for his behavior and choices. Satan considered that the first way to remove him from leadership was to break his fellowship with God. God, being holy, cannot dwell in the midst of dirt and filth. Joshua's unrighteousness was not welcome in God's presence. Joshua had issues. Satan knew this. He knew he had just legal cause. So, he thought he had a closed case against him.

I wonder how Joshua felt as he stood before "the angel of the LORD." Since this is prior to Christ's incarnation, it is a type of Jesus. The angel of the Lord is the second member of the Trinity. He is the advocate. He is the "defense attorney." We have already seen this as Jesus's role in our previous chapters, but, as a reminder,

1 John 2:1–2 says, "My little children, I am writing these things to you so that you may not sin. And if anyone sins, we have an Advocate with the Father, Jesus Christ the righteous; and He Himself is the propitiation for our sins; and not for ours only, but also for those of the whole world."

Satan had met more than his match in Jesus. Because when Satan brought the legitimate accusations against Joshua, Jesus stood His ground. Because God is not bound by time like we are, Jesus was able to impute righteousness to Joshua in that courtroom even though this happened before His death on the cross and His resurrection. Second Corinthians 5:21 hadn't yet taken place in our linear reality, but Jesus is the same, yesterday, and forever (Heb. 13:8).

Even though Joshua was guilty, Satan no longer had a case. Even though Joshua stood there, rank in his own filth, Satan could not pin the charges on him. Even though the devil thought he could stop Joshua's divine destiny in its tracks, Jesus knew another plan. As Galatians 3:13 put it, "Christ redeemed us from the curse of the Law, having become a curse for us—for it is written, 'Cursed is everyone who hangs on a tree.'"

Jesus threw Satan a curve ball in what Satan thought was an open-and-shut case. Satan wasn't aware of the truth in 1 John 1:5–7 which says,

> This is the message we have heard from Him and announce to you, that God is Light, and in Him there is no darkness at all. If we say that we have fellowship with Him and yet walk in the darkness, we lie and do not practice the

truth; but if we walk in the Light as He Himself is in the Light, we have fellowship with one another, and the blood of Jesus His Son cleanses us from all sin.

Satan did not take into consideration that Jesus, as the Advocate, had the power to clean up Joshua right then and there. He didn't know Jesus could impute His righteousness to Joshua so that Joshua would no longer be condemned as guilty of his sins. He didn't know about the truth found in Isaiah 43:25 that states, "I, even I, am the one who wipes out your transgressions for My own sake, and I will not remember your sins."

I imagine Satan had stood tall and proud accusing Joshua. He thought he had him. But Jesus knew otherwise. Jesus knew that all He had to do was say the word and Joshua's dirty clothes would be replaced with clean ones. What's more, Satan didn't realize Joshua would be given another chance. But Joshua had a role to play in that second chance.

Once Joshua's filthy clothes were changed to clean ones, we read about an important next step we all must take when living our lives with kingdom authority. Zechariah 3:6–7 says,

And the angel of the LORD admonished Joshua, saying, "Thus says the LORD of hosts, 'If you will walk in My ways and if you will perform My service, then you will also govern My house and also have charge of My courts, and I will grant you free access among these who are standing here.'"

Joshua had been forgiven of his filth and sin by bringing his guilt to the Lord (1 John 1:9), but he was also commissioned with the charge to walk in the ways of the Lord, and to serve Him. To do so, when he had previously been living in sin, meant he needed to repent. Repentance is not merely an acknowledgment of sin. Repentance involves confessing that you agree with the accusations against you and awareness that you accept the forgiveness for these sins through the shed blood of Jesus Christ. But it doesn't stop there. Repentance is related to direction. It's related to movement. After you have confessed your sins and accepted forgiveness, you must also change directions from where you once were headed and turn toward the other direction of righteousness and goodness.

I often compare repentance to driving on a highway. Let's say you are driving on a highway when you realize you are going the wrong way. You wanted to head north, but somehow you are going south. To repent means to not only recognize and agree with the reality you are going the wrong way, but it also means to take the next available off-ramp and turn around and get back on the right way.

What would you think about someone who was driving and you were in the passenger seat and they said they were going the wrong direction but did nothing to change it? You might scratch your head. If they just kept driving the wrong way and saying things like, "Well, I make mistakes—I'm only human," you would question their commitment to their destination. Similarly, when we are confronted with our own sins and come to Christ for the forgiveness of those sins, and yet make no changes in our lives to stop the sins, Jesus probably scratches His head. He may question our commitment to living with kingdom authority and fulfilling our life purpose. Repentance always involves turning from a wrong direction and going toward the right direction—whether in your thoughts, words, or actions.

Jesus not only cleansed Joshua but He recalled him to his post. In fact, Joshua got more than a recall to his post, he got a promotion. Jesus told him that if he would walk in the ways of the Lord and serve Him, then He would expand the borders of his kingdom influence. That's what I call getting back what the enemy has stolen, and then some!

Jesus did a similar thing for Peter, who publicly denied Him three times. Yet after Peter repented, he was gloriously restored, was recalled into ministry, and exercised kingdom authority to open the doors of the church (Luke 22:31–34; John 21:15–17).

We see a similar thing take place in another biblical story that does not involve individual sin. I want to focus on both situations because there are times in our lives when the difficulties and losses we face are due to our own sin, but there are other times when Satan strips us of what we love due to no fault of our own. We see this show up in the story of Job. I'm not going to spend a lot of time on Job's story since it's a familiar story to most of us. But as a brief recap, Scripture tells us Job was a good man:

> There was a man in the land of Uz whose name was Job; and that man was blameless, upright, fearing God and turning away from evil. Seven sons and three daughters were born

to him. His possessions also were 7,000 sheep, 3,000 camels, 500 yoke of oxen, 500 female donkeys, and very many servants; and that man was the greatest of all the men of the east. His sons used to go and hold a feast in the house of each one on his day, and they would send and invite their three sisters to eat and drink with them. When the days of feasting had completed their cycle, Job would send and consecrate them, rising up early in the morning and offering burnt offerings according to the number of them all; for Job said, "Perhaps my sons have sinned and cursed God in their hearts." Thus Job did continually. (Job 1:1–5)

Job was a kingdom man. He was a committed disciple living out what it means to truly fear God and take Him seriously. Yet not only was he a man of strong faith but he was also a man with a solid family. Job was also a wealthy man who not only looked after his possessions for his own good but also for the good of his family. He led his family spiritually and did everything he could to empower them in this life. He covered them, which is what a real man does. A real man doesn't abandon his family. A kingdom man covers his family spiritually, emotionally, and financially.

Yet as successful as he was, Job was not immune from troubles or trials. In fact, it was due to his success that Satan chose him for targeting. Satan wanted to trip Job up so that Job would eventually get to the point where he lost his faith and cursed God. We read about this in verses 6–11:

Now there was a day when the sons of God came to present themselves before the Lord, and Satan also came among them. The Lord said to Satan, "From where do you come?" Then Satan answered the Lord and said, "From roaming about on the earth and walking around on it." The Lord said to Satan, "Have you considered My servant Job? For there is no one like him on the earth, a blameless and upright man, fearing God and turning away from evil." Then Satan answered the Lord, "Does Job fear God for nothing? Have You not made a hedge about him and his house and all that he has, on every side? You have blessed the work of his hands, and his possessions have increased in the land. But put forth Your hand now and touch all that he has; he will surely curse You to Your face."

Satan and his demons gathered before God to accuse Job ahead of time. They accused him of denying God if he were to suffer loss. He wanted to destroy this man of God, so he asked permission to create devastating situations to take place in Job's life. Eventually, Job would lose all of his children and his possessions. Not only that, but he would also lose his own health. Surely that would be enough, Satan thought. Surely after suffering the loss of what he loved most, he would give up on God. Satan couldn't accuse Job of his actions because he had done no wrong up to that point, or he had made ample sacrifices for any wrongs done. But what he could challenge Job on was his motivation for being so good.

He challenged God to consider that Job only loved Him because Job was extremely blessed by Him. He thought if he removed that blessing and protection from Job's life, then Job would wind up like everyone else. He would doubt God. He would stumble. He would blame. In essence, Satan brought an accusation against Job's motivation for his love for God. That would be something only demonstrable by removing the blessings in Job's life.

God allowed Satan to carry out his plan, but He established a limit to it: "Then the LORD said to Satan, 'Behold, all that he has is in your power, only do not put forth your hand on him.' So Satan departed from the presence of the LORD" (1:12). After this, Job entered into the worst season of his life. Within twenty-four hours, he lost his kids, his business, and his home. Fire consumed everything he had. It wasn't a minor hiccup in Job's life that took place. Satan unleashed a torrent of trials and disasters in a short period of time.

I don't think anyone would have looked down on Job for doubting God after so much pain and loss. But Job knew about the doctrine of sovereignty. He knew his life was not formed by luck, chance, or happenstance. He understood that God allowed it. God never has to say, "Oops, I missed that!" You can't throw God a surprise party! This is important to realize in your own life because when life collapses on you, like it did with Job, if you don't have a handle on the sovereignty of God, you will collapse with it. You won't be able to do what Job did, and that is to worship God. We see this in verses 20–22:

210

Then Job arose and tore his robe and shaved his head, and
he fell to the ground and worshiped. He said,

>"Naked I came from my mother's womb,
>And naked I shall return there.
>The LORD gave and the LORD has taken away.
>Blessed be the name of the LORD."

Through all this Job did not sin nor did he blame God.

We all know that worship comes easy when everything is going
well. But when stuff goes south, it's a lot harder to do. And yet
that's exactly what Job chose to do. He had lost everything dear to
him, and yet he still chose to worship God. It's not that he ignored
his pain. We read he grieved deeply. He tore his robe. He shaved
his head. He fell to the ground in emotional despair. But in the
midst of his loss, he worshipped. He didn't even blame God for
what took place.

There's only one thing that will keep you from blaming God
when you know He could have prevented whatever painful situation that took place in your life. There's only one thing that will
keep you from blaming God when you know He had the power
to heal you or your loved one. There's only one thing that can
hold you back from blaming God when you know He could have
stopped, or reversed, or interfered with whatever Satan was throw-
ing your way. That thing is believing God knows what He is doing
even when the devil is at work. You have to believe God allowed it
for a reason.

Yes, I understand that knowing this spiritual truth doesn't alleviate the heartache, headache, or life ache you feel. But what it does do is keep you from collapsing with everything else all around you. You and I must accept that God is in charge, or we will never make it in a world gone mad. One of the easiest ways to derail a believer from fully using the kingdom authority that is theirs to use is in getting the believer to doubt and blame God. Doubting and blaming God removes a person from proper alignment underneath Him. And, as we've seen throughout this book, alignment is everything when it comes to actualizing spiritual authority.

Job understood that God was in charge. He understood God could have prevented the pain he was going through. But He also knew God had a reason for allowing it. We gain greater insight into Job's thinking in Job 2 when his wife, most likely grieving and in pain herself, tells him to curse God and die. This took place after Satan had returned to God to ask permission to cause bodily pain to Job. Given that permission, Satan covered Job with "sore boils from the sole of his foot to the crown of his head" (Job 2:7).

Seeing her husband in pain, we read his wife's response in verse 9: "Then his wife said to him, 'Do you still hold fast your integrity? Curse God and die!'" Job had not only lost most of his family, all of his business, and his security, he now suffered from a painful debilitation in his health. But instead of cursing God, Job reminded his wife about his trust and faith in God.

Job's response reveals his heart when we read, "But he said to her, 'You speak as one of the foolish women speaks. Shall we indeed accept good from God and not accept adversity? In all this Job did not sin with his lips" (2:10). I know that when my wife of forty-nine years went home to glory after her struggle with cancer, I had to remind myself to focus on what God had given and not on what I had lost. In my grief, I had to thank God for the forty-nine years I did have with Lois. Now, I had to do that with tears and in a lot of pain, but I had to do it because if I were to lose sight of the sovereignty of God, then I would be lost altogether. The same would happen to you if you choose to focus only on the pain and not the provision.

Job didn't know the reason behind his suffering. He didn't know anything about the conversation between God and the devil. That was a private meeting in heaven's courts. In fact, by the time the book ends, Job still doesn't know something is happening up there that's affecting him down here. Far too many of us are unaware of this truth too. There are things going on in the spiritual realm that we will never know about down here. That's why it is so important to be connected to God spiritually and intimately so you can handle the stuff you don't understand. You have to understand whenever you are trying to figure something out that God doesn't allow you to figure out, it's because He doesn't want it to be figured out. There are certain things God chooses to remain hidden (Deut. 29:29). What's more, there are times when He even allows Himself to remain hidden.

Job experienced that as well. In the middle of his life and health collapsing, God was no longer anywhere to be found. Job 23:8–9 says, "Behold, I go forward but He is not there, and backward, but I cannot perceive Him; When He acts on the left, I cannot behold Him; He turns on the right, I cannot see Him." Job was searching for God when his world had been turned upside down, but he could not find him. He was praying to God but there was no known response.

And yet, even then, he did not curse God. His faith remained steadfast. We read in verses 10–12, "But He knows the way I take; When He has tried me, I shall come forth as gold. My foot has held fast to His path; I have kept His way and not turned aside. I have not departed from the command of His lips; I have treasured the words of His mouth more than my necessary food." When you don't hear from God in the middle of your need for God, you need to realize like Job did that you are in the crucible of preparation for recovery. When God goes silent on you and you are suffering, you must keep going. You must keep the faith. You must remain in alignment. If you do, then you will also come forth as pure as gold.

When a goldsmith sets out to purify gold, it is because he wants to remove the dross. He wants to get rid of the alloys. A goldsmith can tell if the gold has become pure because he will be able to clearly see his reflection in it. Similarly, God will often allow a purifying process to take place in our own lives—even though it is painful—so that He can remove the sin, pride, and other contaminants from our lives. God wants to see His pure reflection in our lives. When God can see His own reflection in the crucible of heat He has allowed in our lives, then He knows we are ready for whatever next phase He is about to bring us into.

That's important to remember for those times when you find yourself in the crucible of suffering and you can't find God. It is because there is still something left that God wants to do in you to conform you to the image of Christ (Rom. 8:28–29). Most believers lose out on experiencing and utilizing the kingdom authority that is available to them because they are unable to go through life's pains and seasons of suffering while remaining in alignment with God. Satan knows this is an easy way to derail a believer from living as an effective kingdom disciple, so he uses that technique a lot. But Job provides us with an example of what it looks like to not only go through that time of trials and tribulations, but to come out the other side of it even stronger than before.

One of Job's problems that got addressed through his suffering is that he thought he knew more than he did. It took his pain and loss to teach him that God is bigger, stronger, more powerful than he ever imagined. It took the crucible for Job to get to understand that as he should. We see Job expressing what he learned toward the end of his book in chapter 42:

> Then Job answered the LORD and said,
> "I know that You can do all things,
> And that no purpose of Yours can be thwarted.
> 'Who is this that hides counsel without
> knowledge?'

Therefore I have declared that which I did not
    understand,
Things too wonderful for me, which I did not
    know."
'Hear, now, and I will speak;
I will ask You, and You instruct me.'
"I have heard of You by the hearing of the ear;
But now my eye sees You;
Therefore I retract,
And I repent in dust and ashes." (42:1–6)

Job's view of God changed and expanded as he responded to his pain in a manner of worship and seeking God. He had previously understood God and His principles cognitively, yet through his suffering he learned of God's character and power experientially. There exists a big difference between hearing God and seeing God. Head knowledge is very different than seeing God show up in your everyday reality. Knowing the truth is far from seeing the truth work in front of your own eyes. Satan had set out to defeat Job, but, in the end, Job responded rightly to God in the midst of his pain and Job got a greater glimpse of God and love for God than ever before. How you respond to suffering determines what that suffering will produce in your life. Suffering can lead to bitterness, doubt, and regret. Or, it can lead to worship, spiritual maturity, and humility. The latter will give you access to greater kingdom authority.

God has a purpose for your life, but in order for you to carry out that purpose, you need to see Him for who He truly is. That's why the best thing you can do in the middle of a painful scenario is keep your faith in God. Not only will it get you through, but it will also position you to receive back what the devil had stolen. Job got his fortunes restored. In fact, he got back even more than what he had before. It says,

> The LORD restored the fortunes of Job when he prayed for his friends, and the LORD increased all that Job had two-fold. . . . The LORD blessed the latter days of Job more than his beginning. . . . And Job died, an old man and full of days. (42:10, 12, 17)

An interesting thing to note in the verses we just read is that Job got back his fortunes "when he prayed for his friends." If you've read Job at all, then you know that his friends were unkind to him during his season of suffering. They blamed him. They accused him. They prodded him to doubt God. But it wasn't until Job prayed for those who had made his suffering even more unbearable than it was on his own, that Job received his double portion of blessing from God. The act of praying for his friends who had been so hurtful to him reveals one thing about Job—his heart came through

> Suffering can lead to bitterness, doubt, and regret. Or, it can lead to worship, spiritual maturity, and humility. The latter will give you access to greater kingdom authority.

pure. He didn't resent his friends or blame them. He loved them enough to pray for them. He cared for them enough to minister to them in the midst of his own suffering. He knew their views on God were wrong. He knew their hearts needed to be purified. So instead of asking God for things that would benefit him, he asked God to look out for his friends who obviously needed God more.

Ministering to others in the midst of your pain is one of the surest ways to call down the spiritual authority that is yours to claim. Don't just attend church for only yourself, or attend Bible study groups just for you, or even spend time with God just for you. Consider how being at church, in a study group or praying can help others too. One of the primary ways we are seeking to make this more of a reality in our culture today is through our Kindness in the Culture campaign. In this campaign, we are seeking to equip and encourage millions of people to do at least one intentional act of kindness every week, all year long. In doing this act of kindness, the person is to present the gospel as well as pray for the person they are helping.

I believe that if we can get enough people to live out their faith in this way, we will not only change our atmosphere for good, but we will also strengthen the spiritual walk of those taking part. To do an act of kindness for someone while you yourself are going through a difficulty, because you choose to do it in faith, will strengthen your own walk with God. It will position you like Job, who prayed for his friends, and received back what the enemy had stolen.

We can make a difference in our world today, as well as in our own lives, if we apply the principle found in Romans 12:21, which says, "Do not be overcome by evil, but overcome evil with good." There is a lot of evil swirling around in society these days. But rather than bashing it or blaming it or simply pointing it out, we each have the opportunity to upend it. We have the opportunity to reverse it. We have the opportunity to overcome it. We can do so through intentional good works done through the kingdom authority of Christ and for the glory of God.

CONCLUSION

Time for Doors to Open

 Sometime ago I found myself stuck in my garage because I could not get my garage door to open so I could drive my car to my destination. Pushing the button didn't work in spite of everything being plugged in. Additionally, the door was far too heavy for me to lift. I needed help from outside of myself to open up a door that stayed closed.

In a panic, I called the repairman for help. He instructed me to go to the door and tell him the direction the two canisters at the bottom of the door were pointing. I informed him one was pointed toward the other while the second was pointed straight forward. He informed me that my powerlessness regarding opening my door was because the canisters were out of alignment. They needed to be pointed out to one another so that the door could pick up the signal. When I adjusted the one that was out of alignment and pushed the button, the result was that the door immediately opened, because now it could receive the signal.

When it comes to exercising kingdom authority, too many believers find the door of their deliverance and destiny unable to open and too heavy to lift. But when we make our appeal to the unseen expert in heaven and get in alignment under His rule and obey His Word, we will begin to see the instruction from heaven open up the closed doors on earth so that we begin seeing all that kingdom authority can do for us and through us for the benefit of others.

The Urban Alternative

 The Urban Alternative (TUA) equips, empowers, and unites Christians to impact *individuals, families, churches,* and *communities* through a thoroughly kingdom-agenda worldview. In teaching truth, we seek to transform lives.

The core cause of the problems we face in our personal lives, homes, churches, and societies is a spiritual one; therefore, the only way to address it is spiritually. We've tried a political, social, economic, and even a religious agenda.

It's time for a **kingdom agenda**.

The kingdom agenda can be defined as
the visible manifestation of the comprehensive
rule of God over every area of life.

The unifying central theme throughout the Bible is the glory of God and the advancement of His kingdom. The conjoining thread from Genesis to Revelation—from beginning to end—is focused on one thing: God's glory through advancing God's kingdom.

When you do not recognize that theme, the Bible becomes disconnected stories that are great for inspiration but seem to be unrelated in purpose and direction. Understanding the role of the kingdom in Scripture increases the relevancy of this several-thousand-year-old text to your day-to-day living, because the kingdom is not only then, it is now.

The absence of the kingdom's influence in our personal lives, family lives, churches, and communities has led to a deterioration in our world of immense proportions:

- People live segmented, compartmentalized lives because they lack God's kingdom worldview.
- Families disintegrate because they exist for their own satisfaction rather than for the kingdom.
- Churches are limited in the scope of their impact because they fail to comprehend that the goal of the church is not the church itself, but the kingdom.
- Communities have nowhere to turn to find real solutions for real people who have real problems because the church has become divided, ingrown, and unable to transform the cultural and political landscape in any relevant way.

The kingdom agenda offers us a way to see and live life with a solid hope by optimizing the solutions of heaven. When God is no longer the final and authoritative standard under which all else falls, order and hope leaves with Him. But the reverse of that is true as well: as long as you have God, you have hope. If God is still in the picture, and as long as His agenda is still on the table, it's not over.

Even if relationships collapse, God will sustain you. Even if finances dwindle, God will keep you. Even if dreams die, God will revive you. As long as God, and His rule, are still the overarching standard in your life, family, church, and community, there is always hope.

Our world needs the King's agenda. Our churches need the King's agenda. Our families need the King's agenda.

We've put together a three-part plan to direct us to heal the divisions and strive for unity as we move toward the goal of truly being one nation under God. This three-part plan calls us to assemble with others in unity, address the issues that divide us, and to act together for social impact. Following this plan, we will see individuals, families, churches, and communities transformed as we follow God's kingdom agenda in every area of our lives. You can request this plan by sending an email to info@tonyevans.org or by going online to tonyevans.org.

In many major cities, there is a loop that drivers can take when they want to get somewhere on the other side of the city, but don't necessarily want to head straight through downtown. This loop will take you close enough to the city so that you can see its towering buildings and skyline, but not close enough to actually experience it.

This is precisely what we, as a culture, have done with God. We have put Him on the "loop" of our personal, family, church, and community lives. He's close enough to be at hand should we need Him in an emergency, but far enough away that He can't be the center of who we are.

We want God on the "loop," not the King of the Bible who comes downtown into the very heart of our ways. Leaving God on the "loop" brings about dire consequences as we have seen in our own lives and with others. But when we make God, and His rule, the centerpiece of all we think, do, or say, it is then that we will experience Him in the way He longs for us to experience Him.

He wants us to be kingdom people with kingdom minds set on fulfilling His kingdom's purposes. He wants us to pray, as Jesus did, "not My will, but Yours be done" (Luke 22:42). Because His is the kingdom, the power, and the glory (Matt. 6:13).

There is only one God, and we are not Him. As King and Creator, God calls the shots. It is only when we align ourselves underneath His comprehensive hand that we will access His full power and authority in all spheres of life: personal, familial, ecclesiastical, and governmental.

As we learn how to govern ourselves under God, we then transform the institutions of family, church, and society using a biblically based kingdom worldview.

Under Him, we touch heaven and change earth.

To achieve our goal, we use a variety of strategies, approaches, and resources for reaching and equipping as many people as possible.

Broadcast Media

Millions of individuals experience *The Alternative with Dr. Tony Evans* through the daily radio broadcast playing on nearly **1,400 radio outlets** and in more than **130 countries**. The broadcast can also be seen on several television networks and is available online at tonyevans.org. You can also listen to or view the daily broadcast by downloading the Tony Evans app for free in the App store. More than 30 million message downloads/streams occur each year.

Leadership Training

The Tony Evans Training Center (TETC) facilitates a comprehensive discipleship platform, which provides an educational program that embodies the ministry philosophy of Dr. Tony Evans as expressed through the kingdom agenda. The training courses focus on leadership development and discipleship in the following five tracks:

- Bible and Theology
- Personal Growth

- Family and Relationships
- Church Health and Leadership Development
- Society and Community Impact Strategies

The TETC program includes courses for both local and online students. Furthermore, TETC programming includes coursework for nonstudent attendees. Pastors, Christian leaders, and Christian laity, both local and at a distance, can seek out The Kingdom Agenda Certificate for personal, spiritual, and professional development. For more information, visit: TonyEvansTraining.org.

The Kingdom Agenda Pastors (KAP) provides a *viable network for like-minded pastors* who embrace the kingdom-agenda philosophy. Pastors have the opportunity to go deeper with Dr. Tony Evans as they are given greater biblical knowledge, practical applications, and resources to impact individuals, families, churches, and communities. KAP welcomes *senior and associate pastors* of all churches. KAP also offers an annual Summit held each year in Dallas, with intensive seminars, workshops, and resources. For more information, visit: KAFellowship.org.

Pastors' Wives Ministry, founded by the late Dr. Lois Evans, provides *counsel, encouragement,* and *spiritual resources* for pastors' wives as they serve with their husbands in the ministry. A primary focus of the ministry is the KAP Summit that offers senior pastors' wives a safe place to *reflect, renew,* and *relax* along with training in personal development, spiritual growth, and care for their emotional and physical well-being. For more information, visit: LoisEvans.org.

Kingdom Community Impact

The outreach programs of The Urban Alternative seek to provide positive impact to individuals, churches, families, and communities through a variety of ministries. We see these efforts as necessary to our calling as a ministry and essential to the communities we serve. With training on how to initiate and maintain programs to adopt schools, or provide homeless services, or partner toward unity and justice with the local police precincts, which creates a connection between the police and our community, we, as a ministry, live out God's kingdom agenda according to our *Kingdom Strategy for Community Transformation.*

The Kingdom Strategy for Community Transformation is a three-part plan that equips churches to have a positive impact on their communities for the kingdom of God. It also provides numerous practical suggestions for how this three-part plan can be implemented in your community, and it serves as a blueprint for unifying churches around the common goal of creating a better world for all of us. For more information, visit: TonyEvans.org and click on the link to access the 3-Point Plan. A course for this strategy is also offered online through the Tony Evans Training Center.

Tony Evans Films ushers in positive life change through compelling video-shorts, animation, and feature-length films. We seek to build kingdom disciples through the power of story. We use a variety of platforms for viewer consumption and have more than 120,000,000+ digital views. We also merge video-shorts and film with relevant Bible study materials to bring people to the saving knowledge of Jesus Christ and to strengthen the body of Christ worldwide. *Tony Evans Films* released the first feature-length film, *Kingdom Men Rising*, in April 2019 in more than 800 theaters nationwide, in partnership with Lifeway Films. The second release, *Journey with Jesus*, is in partnership with RightNow Media and was released in theaters in November 2021.

Resource Development

We are fostering lifelong learning partnerships with the people we serve by providing a variety of published materials. Dr. Evans has published more than 125 unique titles based on more than fifty years of preaching whether that is in booklet, book or Bible study format. He also holds the honor of writing and publishing the first full-Bible commentary and study Bible by an African American, released in 2019. This Bible sits in permanent display as a historic release, in The Museum of the Bible in Washington, DC.

For more information, and a complimentary copy of Dr. Evans' devotional newsletter, call (800) 800–3222, write TUA at P. O. Box 4000, Dallas TX, 75208, or visit us online at www.TonyEvans.org.

Notes

1. Portions of this chapter are taken from *The Wonder of the Word: Hearing the Voice of God in Scripture* (Kingdom Pastor's Library) (Chicago, IL: Moody Publishers, 2019), chapter 1. Used by permission.

2. Daniel Merritt, "Voltaire's Prediction, Home, and the Bible Society: Truth or Myth? Further Evidence of Verification," Crossexsamined.org, August 18, 2019, https://crossexamined.org/voltaires-prediction-home-and-the-bible-society-truth-or-myth-further-evidence-of-verification/.

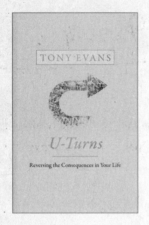

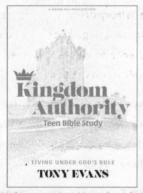
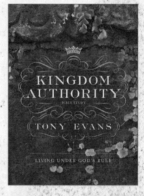

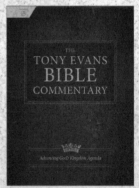

YOUR *Eternity* IS OUR *Priority*

At The Urban Alternative, eternity is our priority—for the individual, the family, the church and the nation. The 45-year teaching ministry of Tony Evans has allowed us to reach a world in need with:

The Alternative – Our flagship radio program brings hope and comfort to an audience of millions on over 1,400 radio outlets across the country.

tonyevans.org – Our library of teaching resources provides solid Bible teaching through the inspirational books and sermons of Tony Evans.

Tony Evans Training Center – Experience the adventure of God's Word with our online classroom, providing at-your-own-pace courses for your PC or mobile device.

Tony Evans app – Packed with audio and video clips, devotionals, Scripture readings and dozens of other tools, the mobile app provides inspiration on-the-go.

**Explore God's kingdom today.
Live for more than the moment.**

Live for *eternity.*

tonyevans.org

Life is busy,
but Bible study is still possible.